THE REGULATION OF MOTOR VEHICLE AND TRAFFIC SAFETY

THE REGULATION OF MOTOR VEHICLE AND TRAFFIC SAFETY

Glenn C. Blomquist

University of Kentucky
Lexington, Kentucky

Kluwer Academic Publishers
Boston/Dordrecht/London

Distributors for North America:
Kluwer Academic Publishers
101 Philip Drive
Assinippi Park
Norwell, Massachusetts 02061 USA

Distributors for the UK and Ireland:
Kluwer Academic Publishers
Falcon House, Queen Square
Lancaster LA1 1RN, UNITED KINGDOM

Distributors for all other countries:
Kluwer Academic Publishers Group
Distribution Centre
Post Office Box 322
3300 AH Dordrecht, THE NETHERLANDS

Library of Congress Cataloging-in-Publication Data

Blomquist, Glenn C.
  The regulation of motor vehicle and traffic safety / Glenn C.
Blomquist.
    p. cm.
  Includes index.
  ISBN 0-89838-280-7
  1. Traffic safety—United States—Cost effectiveness. 2. Traffic
regulations—United States—Cost effectivenss. 3. Automobiles—
Safety measures—Government policy—United States—Cost
effectiveness. I. Title.
HE5614.2.B57   1988   88-15442
363.1′256—dc19   CIP

Cover photograph used with permission from
GTE Corporation.

Printed in the United States of America

CONTENTS

PREFACE

Decisions twenty years ago during the first generation of modern traffic safety policymaking were easier than today. Afterall, the mandate for specific mandatory motor vehicle safety standards was defined rather clearly during legislative hearings. Since the initial standards, decisions have been based on the more general guidelines of "practicality" and avoiding "unreasonable risks." Now, with more difficult decisions pending, the demand for analysis is greater.

My purpose in writing this book is to promote second generation policymaking in traffic safety. The dominant theme is that an "individual net benefit approach" is useful in the design, evaluation and improvement of traffic safety policy. Hopefully, this book provides some guidance for today's tougher decisions.

Evaluative review of modern traffic safety policy, especially automobile safety standards, yields several results. The technological approach, the basis for the 1966 legislation, is shown to produce mistakes. Benefits are overestimated and endangerment of nonoccupants is ignored. The risk homeostatic approach, the devil's idea to some in the safety community, is shown to be a limiting case of the more general individual net benefit approach. Rationality and competency in travelers' safety decisions are reviewed in a broad context. Evidence beyond the realm of behavioral psychology indicates considerable, albeit imperfect, competency in traffic safety decisions. Conventional benefit-cost analysis is critiqued. Existing studies of passive restraints are shown to overestimate net benefits because travelers' responses and costs are ignored. Recommendations are offered as part of an implementation analysis, which balances possible market and policy failures.

Over the years, my ideas concerning the actual effects of appropriate design of traffic safety policy have been shaped by interactions at these notable events:

- The Conference on the Scientific Basis of Health and Safety Regulation, held at the Brookings Institution in 1979;

- The American Enterprise Institute Conference on Health, Safety, and the Environment, held in 1981;

- and more recently my sabbatical at the Swedish Road and Traffic Research Institute in Linköping in 1986.

This book has been improved by interaction with numerous people. For their helpful comments, challenges, and cooperation at various stages and on different parts of this study I am grateful to Kathryn Anderson, Peter Aranson, Philip Berger, Larry Blincoe, Kathleen Blomquist, Orlo Blomquist, Stuart Bretschneider, John Britti, Richard Burkhauser, John Graham, Barry Hirsch, John Hoehn, Marvin Kosters, Peter Linneman, Paul MacAvoy, Michael Mazur, John Mendeloff, John Morrall III, Carl Nash, William Niskanen, Roger Noll, Lloyd Orr, Frank Scott, James Simons, W. Kip Viscusi, Gerald J. Wilde, and three anonymous reviewers for Kluwer Academic Publishers. Comments, challenges and cooperation aside, the views expressed herein are my own. They should not be attributed to the people or to the institutions listed above.

Also, I want to express my appreciation to Elmer Whitler and Cathy Ettinger for preparation of the manuscript for publication and to the James W. Martin School of Public Administration at the University of Kentucky for making their services available for this endeavor. Finally, I thank my family for their support and encouragement. They certainly influence my personal traffic safety decisions.

THE REGULATION OF MOTOR VEHICLE AND TRAFFIC SAFETY

CHAPTER 1

THE MOTOR VEHICLE AND TRAFFIC SAFETY MANDATE

The modern era of safety regulation of motor vehicle travel in the United States began in 1965 with Senate hearings on the federal role in traffic safety. Congressional concern was epitomized in the opening statement by Senator Abraham Ribicoff:

> ...the awful carnage on our roads and streets continues and worsens.... In the past minute 20 accidents have taken place. One-half hour from now three Americans will be dead who right now are alive. And for every half-hour of this day and the days to follow three more human beings will lose their lives on our nation's roads and streets. The preliminary 1964 National Safety Council statistics, which try in hard cold numbers to describe our annual toll of suffering, misery and death resulting from our highways, show that we have again set a record. As a result of traffic accidents which occurred in 1964, 47,800 people have already died, and before the records are closed the total is expected to exceed 48,000 which is 10 percent more than 1963 fatalities which numbered 43,400. What is even more significant is that the deaths per 100 million miles traveled rose from 5.3 in 1962 to 5.5 in 1963 and 5.7 in 1964. [1]

The use of total traffic fatalities and the fatal accident rate to dramatize the problem and the emotional appeal for government regulation of the manufacture and use of automobiles comprise the main lines of argument in Senator Ribicoff's advocacy of a federal automobile safety program. To a great extent the current appeal for traffic safety policy is the same as that put forth over twenty years ago.

A report by the National Highway Traffic Safety Administration begins as follows:

> In 1980 over 51,000 persons were killed and nearly 4 million were injured, about 250,000 of them seriously, in accidents on our nation's highways. The loss of life and bodily injury resulting from these accidents is a major cause of grief and economic hardship for the immediate victims, their families and friends...the purpose of presenting these [and other] costs is to place in perspective the tragic losses resulting from motor vehicle crashes and to provide information for...structuring programs to combat these needless losses.[2]

Although the appeal is unchanged, traffic safety decisions are more difficult now. As we shall see, the mandate for initial vehicle safety standards were rather clearly defined in the legislative hearings of the mid–60's. The mandate for subsequent regulation, however, provides only that standards protect the public against unreasonable risks and be practicable. The purpose of this book is to promote second generation policymaking in traffic safety when the decisions are tougher. In Chapter 2 a general framework for thinking about traffic safety policy is offered. The individual net benefit framework is contrasted with technological and risk homeostatic approaches and is discussed in light of recent evidence on competency in making risky decisions. In Chapter 3 evidence on the contribution of vehicle safety standards to traffic safety is critically reviewed. Early and recent evidence is interpreted using the general net benefit framework and implications for policy are discussed. In Chapter 4 the controversial standard involving mandatory passive restraints is analyzed. The conventional benefit-cost studies, as well as the Supreme Court decisions about various air bags rules, are critiqued in terms of analytical and economic adequacy. Chapters 5 and 6 focus on implementation analysis, which balances possible market and policy failures. Offered are reasons for changing the emphasis of current practice and recommendations for improving traffic safety policy. Broader perspectives are needed organizationally within the Department of Transportation and analytically in regulatory impact analysis.

The remainder of this chapter provides the safety perspective and legislative background for understanding current and prospective policy.

FATALITIES IN TRAFFIC ACCIDENTS – TRENDS AND INCIDENCE

The argument for a traffic safety policy is that motor vehicle traffic accidents are a major cause of death and as such deserve national attention just as do other major causes of death such as heart disease and cancer. [3] The relative importance of traffic fatalities is shown in Table 1-1 for the year 1984. It is apparent that while motor vehicle accidents are the cause of death in only a small share (2.3 percent) of all deaths they do account for a large share (49.8 percent) of accidental deaths. Moreover, other National Safety Council (NSC) statistics for 1983 (Table 1-2) show that motor vehicle accidents are a major cause of death of younger people. For children ages 5 to 14 years 24.9 percent of all deaths are due to motor vehicle accidents. Moreover, the incidence of traffic deaths is noticeably greater for the 5–24 years age group than any other age group shown. For young adults ages 15 to 24 years 38.0 percent of all deaths are due to motor vehicle accidents.

The major youth involvement generates considerable paternalistic demand for an effective traffic safety policy. Paternalism was even greater when the initial hearings were held as the "baby boom" generation was sliding behind the steering wheel to take to the streets and highways. At the time the urgency of the traffic safety problem was indicated by the upward trend in the total number of fatalities in motor vehicle accidents each year up through 1965 and the rise in the annual traffic fatality rate (deaths per 100 million vehicle miles) from 1961 through 1964. As shown in Table 1-3 and Figure 1-1, fatalities increased from 34,763 in 1950 to 38,137 in 1960 to 47,700 in 1964, although there are fluctuations around the trend. [4] The number of fatalities per 100 million vehicle miles decreased steadily from 7.59 in 1950 to 5.16 in 1961 but then increased to 5.63 by 1964. Such was the traffic fatality situation at the start of the hearings leading to the establishment of what are now the National Highway Traffic Safety Administration (NHTSA) and the Federal Highway Administration (FHWA) within the Department of Transportation (DOT). Senator Warren G. Magnuson expressed a popular view that the then pending legislation was so important that it was likely to mark the second session of the 89th Congress as the "Automobile Safety Congress." [5]

Table 1-1   CAUSES OF DEATH, MOTOR VEHICLE ACCIDENTS INCLUDED, 1984

Cause	Number of Deaths	Death Rate [a]	Share of Deaths (%)	Share of Accidental Deaths (%)
All Causes	2,039,369	862.4	100.0	
Heart Disease	765,114	323.5	37.5	
Cancer	453,492	191.8	22.2	
Stroke	154,327	65.3	7.6	
Accidents	92,911	39.3	4.6	100.0
Motor Vehicle	46,263	19.6	2.3	49.8
Falls	11,937	5.0	0.6	12.8
Drowning	5,388	2.3	0.3	5.8
Fires, Burns	5,010	2.1	0.2	5.4
Poison	3,808	1.6	0.2	4.1
Other Accidents	20,505			
Pneumonia	57,798	24.4	2.8	
Diabetis Mellitus	35,787	15.1	1.8	
Suicide	29,286	12.4	1.4	
Chronic Liver Disease	27,317	11.6	1.3	
Arterioschlerosis	24,462	10.3	1.2	
Nephritis and Nephrosis	20,126	8.5	1.0	
Homocide	19,510	8.3	1.0	
Perinatal Conditions	18,881	8.0	0.9	
Other Causes	340,358			

[a] Deaths per 100,000 population

Source: Calculated from National Safety Council, *Accident Facts, 1987 Edition.* (Chicago: NSC, 1987), p. 8.

Table 1-2   INCIDENCE OF MOTOR VEHICLE FATALITIES, BY AGE GROUP, 1984

Age Group (Years)	Deaths	Deaths Due to Motor Vehicle Accidents	Death Rate [a]	Traffic Death Share of Deaths (%)
Under 1	39,580	161	4.5	0.4
1–4	7,372	977	6.9	13.3
5–14	9,076	2,263	6.7	24.9
15–24	38,817	14,738	36.7	38.0
25–44	112,484	15,036	20.9	13.4
45–64	404,568	6,954	15.5	1.7
65–74	476,570	3,020	18.0	0.6
Over 74	950,902	3,114	27.7	0.3
All Ages	2,039,369	46,263	19.6	2.3

[a] Deaths per 100,000 population in age group.

Source: Calculated from National Safety Council, *Accident Facts, 1987 Edition.* (Chicago: NSC, 1987), pp. 8–9.

Table 1-3   TRAFFIC FATALITES AND FATALITY RATES, 1947–1986

Year	Total Fatalites	Annual Change (%)	Fatalities per 100 Million Vehicle Miles	Annual Change(%)	Fatalities per 100 Thousand Population	Annual Change(%)
1947	32,697		8.82		22.8	
1948	32,259	-1.3	8.11	-8.0	22.1	-3.1
1949	31,701	-1.7	7.47	-7.9	21.3	-3.6
1950	34,763	9.7	7.59	1.6	23.0	8.0
1951	36,996	6.4	7.53	-0.8	24.1	4.8
1952	37,794	2.2	7.36	-2.3	24.3	0.8
1953	37,955	0.4	6.97	-5.3	24.0	-1.2
1954	35,586	-6.2	6.33	-9.2	22.1	-7.9
1955	38,426	8.0	6.34	-0.2	23.4	5.9
1956	39,628	3.1	6.28	-0.9	23.7	1.3
1957	38,702	-2.3	5.98	-4.8	22.7	-4.2
1958	36,981	-4.4	5.56	-7.0	21.3	-6.2
1959	37,910	2.5	5.41	-2.7	21.5	0.9
1960	38,137	6.0	5.31	-1.8	21.2	-1.4
1961	38,091	-0.1	5.16	-2.8	20.8	-1.9
1962	40,804	7.1	5.32	3.1	22.0	5.8
1963	43,564	6.8	5.41	1.7	23.1	5.0
1964	47,700	9.5	5.63	4.1	25.0	8.2
1965 [a]	49,163	3.1	5.54	-1.6	25.4	1.6
1966	53,041	7.9	5.70	2.9	27.1	6.7
1967	52,924	-0.2	5.50	-3.5	26.8	-1.1

Year	Total Fatalites	Annual Change (%)	Fatalities per 100 Million Vehicle Miles	Annual Change(%)	Fatalities per 100 Thousand Population	Annual Change(%)
1968 [b]	54,862	3.7	5.40	-1.8	27.5	2.6
1969	55,791	1.7	5.21	-3.5	27.7	0.7
1970	54,633	-2.1	4.88	-6.3	26.8	-3.2
1971	54,381	-0.5	4.57	-6.4	26.3	-1.9
1972	56,278	3.5	4.43	-3.1	26.9	2.3
1973	55,511	-1.4	4.24	-4.3	26.3	-2.2
1974	46,402	-16.4	3.59	-15.3	21.8	-17.1
1975	45,853	-1.2	3.45	-3.9	21.3	-2.3
1976	47,038	2.6	3.33	-3.5	21.6	1.4
1977	49,510	5.3	3.35	0.6	22.5	0.9
1978	52,411	5.9	3.39	1.2	23.6	4.9
1979	53,524	2.1	3.50	3.2	23.8	0.8
1980	53,172	-0.7	3.50	0.0	23.4	-1.7
1981	51,385	-3.4	3.30	-5.7	22.4	-4.3
1982	45,779	-10.9	2.88	-12.7	19.7	-12.1
1983	44,452	-2.9	2.68	-6.9	19.0	-3.6
1984	46,263	4.1	2.69	0.4	19.6	3.2
1985	45,600	-1.4	2.57	-4.5	19.1	-2.6
1986 [c]	47,900	5.0	2.57	0.0	19.9	4.2

[a]Senate hearings on traffic safety commence
[b]Initial FMVSS go into effect
[c]Preliminary estimates
Source: Calculated from National Safety Council, *Accident Facts, 1987 Edition.* (Chicago: NSC, 1987), p. 64–65.

FIGURE 1-1   ANNUAL TRAFFIC FATALITIES AND FATALITY RATES, 1947–1986

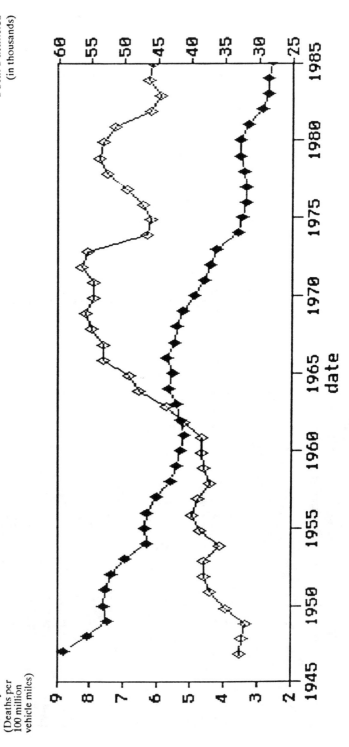

Fatality Rate
(Deaths per
100 million
vehicle miles)

Total Fatalities
(in thousands)

Source: Based on Table 1-3

EARLY CONGRESSIONAL HEARINGS ON TRAFFIC SAFETY

During the Senate and House hearings it was argued that a national traffic safety policy was needed to reduce the number of fatalities. The immediate focus of the debate on motor vehicle safety was on certain safety devices which were to be required on all automobiles purchased by the federal government through the General Services Administration (GSA). The specifications required 17 pieces of equipment. Examples include the following: anchorage for seat belt assemblies, padded dash and visors, impact-absorbing steering wheel and column displacement, safety door latches and hinges, backup lights and outside rear view mirror. [6] The GSA standards were viewed favorably by Senator Ribicoff and others, most notably Daniel P. Moynihan and Ralph Nader. Assistant Secretary of Labor Moynihan advocated a suggestion by William Haddon, Jr., M.D., that a technological approach be taken to traffic accidents. [7]

Dr. Haddon's technological approach holds that there are two crashes in an accident:

- the first collision between the automobile and some external object, and
- the second collision between the occupant and the interior of the automobile.

Furthermore, it holds that it is easier for government to control the second collision, within the automobile, than the first collision. It follows therefore, that the most effective policy is to improve the crashworthiness of the vehicle. Senator Ribicoff emphasized the low cost of improved crashworthiness, e.g., the additional cost of the devices specified by GSA were thought to be between $0 and $90. [8] Ralph Nader summarized the case for Dr. Haddon's technological approach to highway safety in a way which captures what was probably the dominant spirit of the hearings. His testimony reads: "The plain fact is that it is faster, cheaper, and more enduring to build operationally safe and crashworthy automobiles that will prevent death and injury than to build a policy around the impossible goal of having drivers behave perfectly at all times under all conditions in the operation of a basically unsafe vehicle and often treacherous highway conditions." [9] The emphasis is placed on controlling injuries by changing the environment in which the occupant rides, e.g. padding dashboards to reduce head injuries. The emphasis is placed in controlling injuries through engineering improvements, e.g. collapsible steering columns to reduce chest injuries. This emphasis is meant to mitigate the second collision inside the car by relying on a technological approach. Measures designed to mitigate the first collision, in contrast, might focus on enhancing driver performance or redesigning highways to help prevent accidents. [10]

The forthcoming legislation to provide for a national motor vehicle safety policy was justified primarily by testimony such as that described above. The reason given for action by the government was the tragedy of death on the highway. The reason given for motor vehicle safety standards was that they would be effective and inexpensive. The reason for federal pre-emption was the need for quick action to avoid a potential plethora of different state standards, a possibility which made auto manufacturers uneasy. The forthcoming legislation to provide for a national highway safety policy which would deal with motorists and highways was based on similar testimony regarding the tragedy of death on the highway. There was a lively debate, however, on the need for federal standards for highway safety programs. In part the pre-emption issue was whether or not the additional resources from the federal government were worth the loss of states rights to tailor their policies to fit their different circumstances and tastes with respect to highway and traffic safety. Despite the issue of control, the concern for what was perceived to be growing traffic safety problems prevailed.

THE TRAFFIC SAFETY ACTS OF 1966

The National Traffic and Motor Vehicle Safety Act of 1966

On September 9, 1966 Congress enacted Public Law 89–563 which became known as the National Traffic and Motor Vehicle Safety Act of 1966, or simply the Vehicle Safety Act. The purpose, according to the Act, "...is to reduce traffic accident deaths and injuries resulting from traffic accidents...to establish motor vehicle safety standards for motor vehicles and equipment in interstate commerce; to undertake and support necessary safety research and development; and to expand the national driver register." [11]

In prescribing standards the Secretary of Commerce (now Transportation) was expected to consider several factors including:

- "the extent to which such standards will contribute to carrying out the purposes of this Act", and
- "whether any such proposed standard is reasonable, practicable and appropriate for the particular type of motor vehicle or item of motor vehicle equipment for which it is prescribed." [12]

In considering accident and injury research the Act authorized the Secretary to inventory existing research facilities in anticipation of constructing federal facilities for crash tests. The Act also provides for a register to list the names of certain persons who have had their motor vehicle operator's licenses denied, terminated or temporarily withdrawn.[13]

The Highway Safety Act of 1966

A two-pronged attack on the traffic safety problem was made, at least partly, because of what some believed to be an over-emphasis on automobile crashworthiness and design. Anthony J. Celebrezze, Secretary of Health, Education and Welfare; Howard Pyle, President of the National Safety Council, and Frederic G. Donner, Chairman of the Board of General Motors Corporation all testified that the focus on motor vehicle safety standards was too narrow.[14] They argued for a broader approach which recognizes the roles that the driver and road conditions play in accidents. The companion to the Vehicle Safety Act is the Highway Safety Act of 1966 which is an act "...to provide for a coordinated national highway safety program through financial assistance to the states to accelerate highway traffic safety programs..."[15] Programs were expected to include driver education and testing, vehicle registration and inspection, highway design and maintenance, and traffic monitoring and control.[16] In contrast to the Vehicle Safety Act, this Act is designed to lower traffic fatalities by influencing nonvehicle conditions — highway and traffic conditions and driver behavior.

The Vehicle Safety Act and Highway Safety Act are different in other respects. The Vehicle Safety Act provided for regulating the products of a few private motor vehicle manufacturers with little direct effect on the federal budget. The Highway Safety Act provided for regulation of the activities of many, heterogeneous governments with a potentially large direct impact on federal and state budgets. The plan was to create a Federal–State–Local partnership. Both acts provide a mandate for traffic safety policy but the Vehicle Safety Act can be characterized as part of the new "social" regulations nominally intended to protect consumers and workers while the Highway Safety Act is a more traditional intergovernmental grant–public works program.[17] A reading of the congressional hearings leaves the impression that the fervor about automobile crashworthiness did not carry over fully to the highway safety programs.

FEDERAL MOTOR VEHICLE SAFETY STANDARDS

Two months after the Vehicle Safety Act and Highway Safety Act were signed by President Lyndon Johnson, the National Traffic Safety Agency and National Highway Safety Agency were established within the Department of Commerce and William Haddon was appointed as Administrator of both. In April of 1967 the two safety agencies were transferred into the Department of Transportation and three years later became the National Highway Traffic Safety Administration (NHTSA).

Rulemaking, which is thought to be the hallmark of social regulation and motor vehicle safety regulation, began less than a month after the Acts were signed and before the establishment of the Agencies or appointment of the Administrator. By the end of January 1967 all of the following occurred: publication of advance notice of proposed rulemaking in the Federal Register, issuance of notice of proposed rulemaking for 23 vehicle safety standards, industry review of the proposed standards, preparation of final standards, and issuance of 20 final "initial" federal motor vehicle safety standards (FMVSS's). The rulemaking was done in accordance with the Administrative Procedure Act.

The guidelines for the safety standards are contained in the primary legal criteria. The criteria are that the standards should: [18]

- meet the need for motor vehicle safety by protecting the public against **unreasonable risk** of death or injury in the event accidents do occur;
- be stated in terms of **performance** rather than design specifying the required minimum level of performance but not the manner in which it is to be achieved;
- be **practicable** which depends on technical feasibility, production timing and ultimate additional cost (if any) to the consumer; and
- provide **objective** criteria so that compliance can be determined by objective measurement.

There was one additional requirement for the initial standards since they had to be issued by January 31, 1967, and that was that they be based on existing standards. The initial 20 motor vehicle safety standards evolved from 22 voluntary practices recommended by the Society of Automotive Engineers, 19 General Services Administration standards, and standards of the Interstate Commerce Commission, Swedish National Road Board, Uniform Vehicle

Code, Post Office, U.S.A. Standards Institute, state law, and the National Bureau of Standards. [19] The initial 20 standards, shown in Table 1-4 with more recent standards, cover such items as windshield defrosting, hydraulic brake systems and door latches. The initial effective date for almost all of the standards was January 1, 1968. Since 1967, NHTSA has issued 31 additional vehicle safety standards covering such equipment as head restraints, child seating systems, exterior protection (bumpers), pneumatic tires, and motorcycle helmets. Existing standards have been amended with the most notable revision being to Standard No. 208, renamed "Occupant Crash Protection," to include shoulder harnesses, buzzer and light reminders, ignition interlocks, and passive restraints (belts or air bags).

STANDARDS FOR HIGHWAY SAFETY PROGRAMS

The Highway Safety Act provided for federal cooperation with the states in developing approved highway safety programs. Draft proposals for standards were sent by the federal bureau to all Governors, state public health agencies and state highway departments for comments. [20] The National Highway Safety Advisory Committee, established by the Act, made recommendations on the proposals. The resulting standards covered 13 program areas which are now administered by NHTSA and the Federal Highway Administration (FHWA). The programs covered are shown in Table 1-5 and include driver education, drunk driving and highway design.

The standards for each program area were set higher than the least stringent of the state programs with the idea being to set goals toward which the states could work to comply by 1969. States had incentive to implement approved programs in order to get federal highway safety funds and avoid losing 10 percent of their federal-aid highway funds. [21] This financial incentive and the standards in several areas have since changed.

Since the setting of the original highway safety program standards, 5 more standards have been established in the areas of: *Pedestrian Safety*–Std. No. 14, administered by NHTSA and FHWA; *Police Traffic Services*–Std. No. 15, administered by NHTSA, *Debris Hazard Control and Clean-up*–Std. No. 16 administered by NHTSA; *Pupil Transportation Safety*–Std. No. 17, administered by NHTSA; and *Accident Investigation and Reporting*–Std. No. 18, administered by NHTSA. Federal financial assistance for highway safety is provided in the form of 402 funds for safety programs and 403 funds for safety research and development. Funds for highway safety programs are made

Table 1-4 FEDERAL MOTOR VEHICLE SAFETY STANDARDS

Date Issued	Standard Number	General Description	Basis of Initial Standards
January 1967	101	Control Location and Identification	Federal Std. No. 515/3a (GSA)
January 1967	102	Transmission Shift Lever Sequence, Starter Interlock and Transmission	Federal Std. No. 515/11 (GSA)
January 1967	103	Windshield Defrosting and Defogging	*SAE Practice J902
January 1967	104	Windshield Wiping and Washing Systems	Federal Std. No. 515/12a (GSA) and SAE Practices J903a and J942)
January 1967	105	Hydraulic Service Brake, Emergency Brake, and Parking Brake Systems	Federal Std. No. 515/9a (GSA), SAE Practices J937, J843a, and Post Office POD-T-173
January 1967	106	Hydraulic Brake Hoses	SAE Standard J40b
January 1967	107	Reflecting Surfaces	Federal Std. No. 515/13a (GSA)
January 1967	108	Lamps, Reflective Devices and Associated Equipment	ICC Vehicle Lighting Regulatons and various Uniform Vehicle Code, GSA and SAE standards
January 1967	111	Rearview Mirrors	Federal Std No. 515/17a (GSA) and Swedish National Road Board Std.
January 1967	201	Occupant Protection in Interior Impact	Federal Std. No. 515/2a (GSA)

Date Issued	Standard Number	General Description	Basis for Initial Standards
January 1967	203	Impact Protection for the Driver from the Steering Control System	Federal Std. No. 515/4a (GSA)
January 1967	204	Steering Control Rearward Displacement	Federal Std. No. 515/4a (GSA)
January 1967	205	Glazing Materials	Federal Std. No. 515/8 (GSA), based on existing codes
January 1967	206	Door Latches and Door Hinge Systems	Federal Std. No. 515/5a (GSA)
January 1967	207	Anchorage of Seats	Federal Std. No. 515/6a (GSA) and SAE Practice J879
January 1967	208	Seat Belt Installations	Laws of 32 states
January 1967	209	Seat Belt Assemblies	National Bureau of Standards
January 1967	210	Seat Belt Assembly Anchorages	Federal Std. No. 515/1a (GSA) and Nat'l. Bureau of Standards Standard
January 1967	211	Wheel Nuts, Wheel Discs, and Hub Caps	Swedish Nat'l. Road Board Standard
January 1967	301	Fuel Tanks, Fuel Tank Filler Caps, and Fuel Tank Connections	Federal Std. No. 515/26
November 1967	109	New Pneumatic Tires	
November 1967	110	Tire Selection and Rims	
February 1968	202	Head Restraints	

Date Issued	Standard Number	General Description
April 1968	112	Headlamp Concealment Devices
April 1968	113	Hood Latch Systems
April 1968	114	Theft Protection
July 1968	115	Vehicle Identification Numbers
August 1968	212	Windshield Mounting
December 1968	116	Motor Vehicle Brake Fluids
March 1970	213	Child Seating Systems
July 1970	118	Power-Operated Window Systems
October 1970	214	Side Door Strength
December 1970	302	Flammability of Interior Materials
Febraury 1971	121	Air Brake Systems
April 1971	215	Exterior Protection (Bumpers)
April 1971	117	Retreaded Pneumatic Tires
December 1971	216	Roof Crush Resistance
March 1972	122	Motorcycle Brake Systems
March 1972	125	Warning Devices.

Date Issued	Standard Number	General Description
March 1972	124	Accelerator Control Systems
April 1972	123	Motorcycle Controls and Displays
May 1972	217	Bus Window Retention and Release
August 1972	126	Truck-Camper Loading.
August 1972	218	Motorcycle Helmets
November 1973	119	New Pneumatic Tires
June 1975	219	Windshield Zone Intrusion
January 1976	120	Tire Selection and Rims for Vehicles other than Passenger Cars
January 1976	220	School Bus Rollover Protection
January 1976	221	School Bus Body Joint Strength
January 1976	222	School Bus Seating and Crash Protection
March 1978	127	Speedometers and Odometers

Note: Standards typically had an initial effective date of approximately one year after the date issued.

Source: Adapted form U.S. Department of Commerce, National Traffic Safety Agency. *Report on the Development of the Initial Federal Motor Vehicle Safety Standards*. (Washington, D.C.: GPO, March 17, 1967) and U.S. Department of Transportation. NHSTSA. *Motor Vehicle Safety 1979.* DOT HS 624, Dec. 1980, pp .57–59.

Table 1-5   **STANDARDS FOR HIGHWAY SAFETY PROGRAMS**

Standard Number	General Description
1	Driver education and specified universal availability to youths (Now Std. No. 4, NHTSA)
2	Driver licensing and specified universal initial examinations and checks of a driver's record (Now Std. No. 5, NHTSA)
3	Motorcycle safety and specified special licensing and mandatory helmet use (Now Std. No. 3, NHTSA)
4	Traffic records and specified information on vehicles, drivers, and accidents (Now Std. No. 10, NHTSA)
5	Alcohol in relation to highway safety and specified chemical-test procedures for blood-alcohol concentrations and implied consent for testing (Now Std. No. 8, NHTSA)
6	Periodic motor vehicle inspection and specified annual inspections by certified personnel (Now Std. No. 1, NHTSA)
7	Motor vehicle registration and specified data for rapid identification of each vehicle and owner for safety research. (Now Std. No. 2, NHTSA)
8	Highway design, construction, and maintenance and specified design standards for curvature, lane width, lighting, resurfacing, and hazard identification (Now Std. No. 12, FHWA)
9	Traffic control devices and specified uniform signs and signals and speed zone management (Now Std. No. 13, FHWA)

Standard Number	General Description
10	Identification and surveillance of accident locations and specified inventories of high accident locations (Now Std. No. 9, FHWA)
11	Codes and laws and specified uniform rules of the road within each state (Now Std. No. 6, NHTSA)
12	Traffic courts and specified reporting to the state of all moving traffic violations (Now Std. No. 7, NHTSA)
13	Emergency medical services and specified training for ambulance operators, two-way communications and comprehensive planning (Now Std. No. 11, NHTSA)

Source: U.S. Department of Transportation, National Highway Safety Bureau, *Report on Highway Safety Program Standards*. (Washington, D.C.: GPO, July 1, 1967).

available on a 75%/25% federal/state matching basis and prorated by population and road mileage. [22] Recently there is renewed interest in highway safety programs. Programs designed to combat drunken driving, promote seat belt use and improve driver licensing are featured traffic safety activities now. After years of focus on motor vehicle safety standards there is a greater emphasis on influencing driver behavior through highway safety programs and on other safety activities.

OTHER SAFETY ACTIVITIES

Research

The National Highway Traffic Safety Administration has engaged in various safety activities in addition to the promulgation of FMVSS and highway safety program standards. [23] One of these activities is the development of research safety vehicles such as the one developed by Minicars, Inc. The objective is to evaluate performance of experimental vehicles with regard to crash protection, fuel economy, crash avoidance, pedestrian hazard, susceptibility to damage, and marketability. In addition to automatic air bag restraints the cars are equipped with a small radar system which automatically applies the brakes if seemingly unavoidable collisions are detected. Another activity is the operation of Vehicle Research and Test Center in Ohio which is NHTSA's in-house test facility for long-term exploratory research and quick investigations in support of rulemaking.

The safety research for NHTSA is done mostly through grants and contracts to private industry and universities. A considerable portion of the research involves gathering accident data in order to have a better idea of what is actually occurring. Other research investigates crashworthiness of cars, crash survivability, seat belt use, the impairing effects of alcohol and drug use on drivers, public acceptance of the amended national 55 mph speed limit, and motorcycle and pedestrian safety.

The Motor Vehicle Information and Cost Savings Act of 1972

This act requires that NHTSA publish car safety ratings by make and model to increase consumer awareness and foster manufacturer competition to produce more safety. Ratings are based on crashworthiness, damage susceptibility and ease of repair. A related effort was to develop a bumper standard to reduce damage in low-speed impacts. Under the 1966 mandate

NHTSA has also developed the Uniform Tire Quality Grading System to rate the performance of new tires.[24]

Recalls

Under the provisions of the Vehicle Safety Act manufacturers are required to notify consumers and NHTSA of safety defects and the proposed remedy. Since 1966 more than 88 million vehicles have been recalled. Most recalls have been initiated by manufacturers without formal NHTSA involvement. Letters and phone calls from car owners are the primary source of information for defect investigations.[25] As with highway safety programs activity has increased in the recall program in recent years.

PERSPECTIVES

After over 14 years of almost steady decline in the traffic fatality rate (fatalities per 100 million vehicle miles) the fatality rate rose over 9 percent from 1961 to 1964. Traffic fatalities rose over 25 percent during the same 3 year period with a disproportionately large involvement of young drivers. Public concern precipitated congressional hearings which led to the passage of the National Traffic and Motor Vehicle Safety Act of 1966 and the Highway Safety Act of 1966. The Vehicle Safety Act represented the new social regulatory approach to the traffic safety problem through promulgation of Federal Motor Vehicle Safety Standards. The standards are designed to improve automobile crashworthiness and avoid injury due to the "second collision." The Highway Safety Act focused on highway design, traffic control and driver behavior using a more traditional approach of federal grants to states and public works programs. Both acts provided a mandate to improve traffic safety. Twenty FMVSS's based on existing industry practice as well as 13 highway safety program standards were quickly set in place. These first steps were relatively easy especially compared to identifying additional FMVSS's which were "practicable" and protected vehicle occupants from "unreasonable risk."

The attempt here has been to provide a thumbnail sketch of the shaping of the initial traffic safety mandate with some attention given to its current form. Since 1966 the regulatory environment has been shaped by such factors as the energy crunch with the national 55 m.p.h. speed limit and transition to small cars, the Viet Nam War, Watergate, the slowdown in growth of real gross national product, large losses of U.S. automobile manufacturers,

environmental concern, Medicare and Medicaid, and regulatory reforms. [26]
Traffic safety policy has been formulated and implemented by administrations
of five Presidents from Lyndon Johnson to Ronald Reagan and influenced by
testimony given at public, congressional and court hearings. The original
mandate remains but it has been broadened to give greater emphasis to
nonfatal accidents, pecuniary costs of accidents and recalls of defective
vehicles and equipment. Still considerable attention centers on the
implementation of the requirement for passive restraints or alternative state
laws which require safety belt use.

The remainder of this book will examine the traffic safety policy of the last
twenty years, evaluating especially the contribution of federal standards for
vehicle crashworthiness — the new approach which regulates the design and
construction of automobiles.

NOTES

[1] U. S. Congress. Senate. Committee on Government Operations. *Federal Role in Traffic Safety*. Hearings before a subcommittee on Executive Reorganization. 89th Congress, 1st Session, 1965, Part 1, p. 2.

[2] U. S. Department of Transportation. National Highway Traffic Safety Administration. *The Economic Cost to Society of Motor Vehicle Accidents*. DOT HS 806 342. January 1983, pp. I-1 and I-2.

[3] Traffic safety, motor vehicle safety and highway safety are used as three distinct, but related terms in this study. Motor vehicle safety pertains to the design, construction and performance of motor vehicles or equipment i.e., crashworthiness and crash avoidance characteristics. Highway safety pertains to roadway design and maintenance, driver performance and traffic control. Traffic safety is a broad concept which encompasses motor vehicle safety and highway safety and is used in spirit of the general concern about accidents expressed in the congressional hearings of 1965 and 1966.

[4] Table 1-3 shows traffic fatality data reported by the National Safety Council and is based upon death within one year of the accident. Assembling a series of fatality data covering a long period of time is somewhat problematic because of definitioned changes. NHTSA currently reports fatality data based upon death within 30 days of the accident. Using this shorter period reduces the number of fatalities attributed to traffic accidents—by approximately 4 percent. The annual percentage change, however, is affected little by this redefinition. For the FARS data used by NHTSA see U.S. Department of Transportation, National Highway Traffic Safety Administration. *Fatal Accident Reporting System 1984*. DOT HS 806 919, 1984.
We take for granted the quality of the data on fatalities, but some error is inevitable. Attributing deaths to traffic accidents is somewhat arbitrary in cases in which the drivers have heart attacks. Estimates of the deaths per vehicle depend on imprecise estimates of miles traveled.

[5] Senator Magnuson's view is found in U.S. Congress. Senate. Committee on Commerce, *Traffic Safety Hearings*. 89th Congress, 2nd Session, 1966, p. 1. Also, it is interesting to note that from 1947 to 1985 the fatality rate has declined from 8.82 to 2.58 fatalities per 100 million vehicle miles. Approximately 53 percent of the 6.24 decline came between 1947 and 1965 and 47 percent of the decline came in the period 1965 to 1985.

[6] A complete list of the GSA standards can be found in U.S. Congress. Senate. Committee on Government Operations. *Federal Role in Traffic Safety.* Hearings before a subcommittee on Executive Reorganization. 89th Congress, 1st Session, 1965, Part I, p. 201.

[7] Ibid., pp. 283 and 317.

[8] Ibid., Part 2, pp. 672–675.

[9] Ibid., Part 3, 1966, p. 1283. Nader elaborates on his view in his book *Unsafe at Any Speed* (New York: Grossman Publishers, 1965). He argues that the design of the Corvair was a major factor contributing to automobile accidents involving that car model.

[10] Haddon couched his recommendations in terms of epidemiology and Nader couched his recommendations in terms of engineering design. Both of these interested parties advocated emphasis on what will be called a "technological" approach to increasing traffic safety by increasing crashworthiness. Their approach seeks a technological fix and ignores motorist behavior.

[11] U.S. Congress. *National Traffic and Motor Vehicle Safety Act of 1966.* Public Law 89–563. 89th Congress, 2nd Session, 1966, Introduction.

[12] Ibid., Sec. 103.

[13] Ibid., Secs. 301, 302 and 401.

[14] For testimony see U.S. Congress, Senate, Committee on Government Operations. *Federal Role in Traffic Safety* Part 1, 1965, p. 215; Part 2, 1965, p. 654 and Part 3, 1966, p. 1107.

[15] U.S. Congress. *Highway Safety Act of 1966.* Public Law 89–564. 89th Congress, 2nd Session, 1966, Introduction.

[16] Ibid., Sec. 402.

[17] Traditional regulation deals with retail markets and focuses on rate structure and service delivery. New-style, social regulation deals with health, safety and the environment and focuses on protecting the consumer. For

elaboration on the difference see William Lilley III and James C. Miller III. *The New "Social Regulation" Washington, D.C., American Enterprise Institute* Reprint No. 66, May 1977 and Paul W. MacAvoy *The Regulated Industries and the Economy* (New York: W. W. Norton & Co., 1979).

[18] U.S. Department of Commerce. National Traffic Safety Agency. *Report on the Development of the Initial Federal Motor Vehicle Safety Standards* (Washington, D.C.: GPO, March 17, 1967) pp. 5–11.

[19] Ibid., p. iii.

[20] See U.S. Department of Transportation. National Highway Safety Bureau. *Report on the Highway Safety Program Standards* (Washington, D.C.: GPO, July 1, 1967).

[21] Ibid., p. 14.

[22] U.S. Department of Transportation. National Highway Traffic Safety Administration. *Highway Safety 1980.* DOT HS 806 308, Nov. 1982.

[23] For descriptions of other safety activities see the U.S. Department of Transportation, NHTSA, annual reports titled *Highway Safety* and *Motor Vehicle Safety.*

[24] The Energy Policy and Conservation Act of 1975 requires NHTSA to set average fuel economy standards for motor vehicles. While this may be an important activity for NHTSA it is not specifically a safety program.

[25] U.S. Department of Transportation. NHTSA. *Motor Vehicle Safety 1980* DOT HS 806 309, Nov. 1982, pp. 17, 25, 27, 34–37.

[26] The changing economic and regulatory environment has proved to be a formidable challenge for public policy. For example, Lester Lave argues current federal regulation of automobile safety, emissions and fuel economy is contradictory. One reason is that the regulations are designed one at a time ignoring interaction and multiple goals. See Robert W. Crandall, Howard K. Gruenspecht, Theodore E. Keeler and Lester B. Lave *Regulating the Automobile* (Washington, D.C.: The Brookings Institution, 1986), Chapter 7.

CHAPTER 2
A FRAMEWORK FOR THINKING ABOUT TRAFFIC SAFETY POLICY

THE NATURE OF THE MANDATE

The Vehicle Safety Act and the Highway Safety Act of 1966 were the legislative results of a successful appeal to do something about the sharp increase in what was referred to as the awful carnage on the nation's roads and streets. The traffic safety mandate was based on the premise that anything which causes thousands of deaths and injuries each year deserves national attention. Melvin Bergheim of Americans for Democratic Action, appearing before the House Committee on Interstate and Foreign Commerce, articulated this premise. He asserted that consumers have a right to expect that their government will protect them from harm. He argued that there is an army to protect from outside aggression, a police force to protect from crime, a public health service to protect from disease and there is nothing fundamentally different philosophically about asking the government to protect from slaughter on the highways.[1]

The mandate from the Vehicle Safety Act was to reduce traffic deaths and injuries by establishing vehicle safety standards which were practicable, objective and stated in terms of performance. The vehicle safety standards presumably protect the public against unreasonable risk. The mandate from the Highway Safety Act was to reduce traffic deaths and injuries by assisting the states with programs to improve the performance of drivers and pedestrians and the design of highways. The directions were quite clear for the initial 20 vehicle safety standards and 13 highway safety program standards. The suggestions for future policy actions, in contrast, were essentially symbolic in nature. Consider the wide latitude given in determining when the risk of death is "unreasonable," when a standard is "practicable" or when highway design is sufficiently "improved." During the ensuing discussions about the desirability of proposed standards what approach was to be used in making allocative decisions? The technological approach prevailed.

THE TECHNOLOGICAL APPROACH

During the early Congressional hearings on safety William Haddon, Jr., M.D., who became the first Administrator of both the National Traffic Safety Agency and the National Highway Safety Agency, advocated that a technological approach to traffic fatalities and injuries be taken.[2] According to his approach there are two crashes in an accident:

- the first collision between the automobile and some external object, and
- the second collision between the occupant and the interior of the automobile.

Furthermore, the technological approach holds that the second collision, within the automobile, is easier to control than the first collision, which involves driver behavior.

The application of this technological approach treats people as passive in that it is assumed that roadway users do not respond to changes in the traffic environment. Such an application implies that regulations which promote safety through more crashworthy vehicles do not affect the number or severity of traffic accidents. For example, according to this approach the annual safety benefits of a Federal Motor Vehicle Safety Standard, such as FMVSS No. 208 requiring passive restraints, are estimated in two steps. The first is to estimate the intrinsic efficacy or safety productivity of passive belts and air bags through lab tests or through studies by crash investigation teams. They determine what fraction of the occupants would survive different types of accidents with passive restraints. The second is to multiply the efficacy times the number of accidents of each type which would occur. Previous accident rates are assumed to be good estimates of the rates which will be experienced with the safety standard. The distribution of accidents by severity is determined exogenously. Undoubtedly, the popularity of the technological approach is due to its simplicity and appeal as a quick fix. The approach is simple in that the policy should focus on changes in vehicle and highway design, not the behavior of roadway users. Policy benefits derive from the reduction in fatal or injury risk given a crash occurs—the intrinsic effect of the accident countermeasure.[3]

THE RISK HOMEOSTATIC APPROACH

Underlying the formulation of traffic safety policy is an explicit or implicit model of human behavior concerning traffic safety and response to traffic policy. The prevailing policy approach, at least initially, was one based on passive roadway users. If we doubt perfect passivity, then we should wonder if an approach and research technique well suited to laboratory and clinical setting (the technological approach) is being misapplied to traffic safety with undue ad hoc modifications.

The risk homeostatic approach rejects perfect passivity and in contrast to the technological approach focuses instead on human response to environmental change when the personal target level of risk is unchanged. Risk homeostasis was developed, according to its author Gerald J. S. Wilde, because in the domain of psychological research there is a sparsity of comprehensive and articulate conceptions about human behavior and traffic safety. Wilde partly fills this void by providing a task analysis model in which the roadway user is understood to behave according to a homeostatically controlled, self-regulation process.[4] At any moment in time the roadway user, perhaps a driver, compares the perceived risk being experienced with the target level of risk which the driver wishes to achieve. Whenever a discrepancy is perceived decisions are made as to whether or not to take action to eliminate the difference. If the perceived safety risk level is greater than the target safety risk level, then the driver will take action (for example, brake) in order to reduce the risk level. If the perceived risk level is greater than the target risk level then the driver will take action (for example, speed up) in order to save time and increase the risk level. The ability to maintain the constant, target risk level depends on perceptual skills, decisional skills and vehicle handling (executional) skills.

This model of the dynamics of human conduct in the face of risk has a direct implication for traffic safety policy. Vehicle safety standards will have at most only a temporary effect on subjective or objective risk and hence only a temporary effect on traffic fatalities rates (or other measures) unless there is a change in the personal target levels of risk. The target level of risk is determined by drivers' perceptions of the benefits and costs of risky and cautious behavior. Risk homeostasis implies that policy must be directed at the target levels of risk chosen by roadway users if policy is to have long lasting effects on safety.[5] Human behavior is the dominant force in the risk homeostatic approach. Technological changes will be completely offset by user response unless the target level of risk is changed.

A GENERAL FRAMEWORK:
THE INDIVIDUAL BENEFIT-COST APPROACH

The Individual Benefit-Cost Approach

The technological approach can produce useful estimates of intrinsic safety effects, but in general it is misleading because roadway users are assumed to be perfectly passive to changes in the traffic environment. The risk homeostatic approach provides cognitive plausibility to human response to changes in the safety environment, but it is incomplete because of the emphasis on psycho-physiological arousal and not the choice of targets. To understand traffic safety we need an approach which neither precludes response of roadway users nor precludes changes in target levels of safety. We should have an approach which allows for interactions among design features of motor vehicles, construction characteristics of highways and the short-term responses and long-term goals of travelers who use them. Such a comprehensive approach is essential to balanced, systematic formulation, evaluation and implementation of traffic safety policy. We shall call this approach the individual benefit-cost approach, or individual net benefit approach for short. The focus is on the choice of the target level of safety and the choice of ways of achieving the target level.

The starting point is the acknowledgment that roadway users have some control over their own accident risks and that it is these individuals more than anyone else who have the most at stake in decisions concerning their own traffic safety. To assume that accident risk is partly endogenous is to say, for example, that drivers can affect intrinsic safety through the choice of vehicle and can affect also the probability that an accident occurs through the manner in which any chosen vehicle is operated. To assume that individuals care the most about their own safety is to say that the survival instinct is basic.

The general framework is that individuals pursue safety and nonsafety goals and use their resources and arrange their activities so as to get as much overall satisfaction as humanly possible.[6] In other words, roadway users maximize their expected utility given their limited budgets, technology, and the safety environment. Roadway users balance goals and weigh actions which affect their own traffic safety in terms of the expected private benefits and costs. The benefits depend on the roadway users' own values of good health and others' care for and dependency on them. Benefits depend on the users' avoidance of medical expenses, vehicle repair costs, liability lawsuits and increases in insurance rates. The costs depend on the time, care and effort involved, the equipment purchased and their values. Driving at moderate speeds, responding to changing weather conditions, staying well-rested and sober are examples of what can be done by a driver who wants more traffic safety. Roadworthy tires, toll roads and sound vehicles can be purchased by drivers who desire more traffic safety. Publicly-provided items such as traffic rules, highway design and vehicle regulations can affect individuals' benefits and costs.

The optimal amount of traffic safety reflects individuals' valuations of the advantage and disadvantages associated with traffic safety and changes in traffic safety. The desired, or target, level of traffic safety chosen by the individual roadway user depends on both benefit factors and cost factors including those which are publicly provided. Again consider an important user, the driver. When drivers find themselves facing too much risk, they respond by purchasing better tires or taking more rest stops while driving at night. When drivers find themselves giving up too much of nonsafety desirables, such as clothing for their children, they try to get a few more miles out of the old tires. Individual benefits and costs are reflected in this behavior.

Implications for Traffic Safety Policy

The individual benefit-cost framework is a more general framework than either the technological or risk homeostatic approaches and as a consequence it has broader implications for traffic safety policy. In policy practice the focus of the technological approach is on the design of effective, safety devices with the goal of increasing traffic safety as much as possible. In policy practice the focus of the risk homeostatic approach is on the offsetting response of roadway users to interventions and the inevitable implementation problems which reduce the effectiveness of mandated design changes. The assumption of passive people is rejected but goal of increasing traffic safety is not.

The individual net benefit framework focuses on the choice of target levels of safety by individual roadway users with the goal of good, individual traffic safety decisions. A direct implication is no traffic safety policy is appropriate if individuals make good safety decisions. If the decisions are poor, then attention is given to determining how poor and to ways to improve them. If the decisions are good enough, then no policy action is necessary. This more general framework is the most unsettling of the approaches to traffic safety because it requires not only consideration of human response to policy measures but also consideration of the wisdom of increasing safety as much as possible. The wisdom depends partly on the quality of individual decisions.

POTENTIAL IMPERFECTIONS IN MOTORISTS DECISIONS: TYPES AND EVIDENCE

Insufficient Incentives

A social problem may arise if in choosing their target levels of safety individual travelers fail to take into account fully any benefits or costs accruing to others. If effects external to individuals, externalities, exist and they are not considered by the individuals, then the resulting level of traffic safety will be inappropriate for society as a whole. The policy concern is that motorists are not safe enough because of external benefits of safety (external costs of accidents) which they ignore.

Individual demand for traffic safety partly depends on avoiding the payment of medical expenses which will result from a traffic accident. While some outlay of money and time can be expected with each accident the outlay may be less than the total accident-related medical expense because of community-rated health insurance premiums or public assistance-related third party financing such as Medicaid and Medicare. The potential shift of some medical costs to those not involved in an accident means that individual demand for traffic safety tends to be too low. Similarly the demand may be too low because of the lack of precise experience rating for automobile insurance and possibly incomplete compensation for damaged parties through the courts especially when time costs and death are involved.

Clearly these financial externalities do exist. We should be skeptical, however, of claims that these completely ruin individual safety choices. Fatal accident risks generate policy concern, but externalities seem to be small relative to the values that individuals place on reducing their own fatality risks. Recent estimates indicate that individuals are willing to pay approximately

$100 per year to reduce their risk of death by 1 in 10,000. This implies a value of statistical life of approximately $1 million.[7] This individually perceived benefit is substantial. Also we do have some idea of the percentage by which this individual value differs from the social value, which considers the benefits to others as well as the benefit to the individual. In a study of willingness to pay values useful for public benefit-cost analysis, Martin Bailey estimated that due to financial externalities the social value exceeds individual value an average of 18%. We could also use the dubious measure, foregone labor earnings, for the individual's own value and calculate the externality based on the estimates of NHTSA for what would be external costs. If we did we would find for fatal accidents the difference is 13 percent. The difference is due to others' share of medical costs, property damage, legal and court costs, coroner costs, emergency cost, insurance expense, public assistance administration and government programs.[8] If we used the preferred willingness to pay values instead of earnings the difference would be an even smaller percentage. Claims of large estimates are exaggerated. The exaggeration is due to the failure to recognize that individuals place considerable value on their own lives and take these values into account when making their own traffic safety decisions. If we recognize that travelers are choosing target levels of safety and that they value their own lives greatly, then it is the external benefits not the total benefits which suggest the need for a safety policy intervention. Within our individual cost framework we can see the case for an active traffic safety policy is overstated by Nelson Hartunian and others who mistakenly emphasize total rather than external benefits.[9]

One can interpret some federal traffic safety activities as measures to counter insufficient incentives. Most of these activities are part of the highway safety programs resulting from the Highway Safety Act. Recently there has been a marked interest in reducing the contribution of drunk driving to traffic accidents by increasing the incentive to stay sober while driving. Three of the four key areas designated to receive additional funds are alcohol safety (Standard No. 8), police traffic services (Standard No. 15) and traffic records (Standard No. 10). Other developments such as no-fault automobile insurance and greater third party financing of health costs have the opposite effect of decreasing incentives and demand for safety. Nonetheless the external benefits and costs appear small compared to incentives the individuals have for themselves.

Insufficient Information

Travelers themselves may have the most to gain from traffic safety or lose from traffic accidents, but they may not behave accordingly if they do not have enough information about the benefits and costs of safety. Presumably drivers have some idea of how speed, alcohol consumption, rest stops, clean windshields, safety belts, vehicle design, tire wear, vehicle maintenance, weather conditions, traffic conditions, and road conditions affect the risks of accident and injury. Some of this information pertains to all drivers, not just an individual so that once one driver learns of these effects other drivers could benefit from the individual's learning as well. Such publicness of safety information could lead to under-provision of safety information and poor safety decisions. The lack of sufficient information could cause individuals to choose too little safety and later regret the choice when better information is obtained. While insufficient information is a potential safety problem, considerable information is available now.

Private sources of information do exist including *Consumer Reports, Car and Driver,* analytical and daily news articles, driving schools and word-of-mouth. Public sources of information include driver education in public schools, the NHTSA toll-free Auto Safety Hotline, safety defect investigations and recalls, and *The Car Book.*[10] These sources can be viewed as efforts to supply more information to individuals so that they can make good decisions and thereby produce a socially optimal amount of traffic safety. While existing programs might be improved, it appears that individual travelers do have a great deal of information. Assertions that roadway users are making decisions without information which is relevant to their travel must be evaluated recognizing that many commercial, private and public sources already exist. Any comparison to a transport world without any safety information at all is irrelevant for current policy.

Insufficient Competency

Even if travelers fully consider all benefits and costs of their actions and are well-informed a social safety problem may arise if individuals cannot process properly information about risks. The individual benefit-cost approach sees people who can evaluate the target level of safety which they have chosen. The approach sees people who have the ability to compare their subjective estimates of risk being experienced to their target level and respond to any gap between the two. The criticism of safety decisions which we should take most seriously is the challenge to individual competency.

One challenge is to people's ability to perceive risks. An example would be drivers who believe that their own driving skills are so superior that they perceive their risk to be so low that they would not respond to any changes in risk. Competent drivers would respond to changes. The basis for the criticism of perceptual skills are the studies of "behavioral" psychologists who find limits to people's ability to perceive all risks accurately.[11]

Another challenge goes beyond perceptual incompetence to criticize any expected utility approach including our individual net benefit approach. Herbert Simon challenged the approach by arguing that people have limited time, information, capacity to process information and limited ability to compute outcomes. "Bounded rationality" compels people to simplify decision making problems and focus on some aspects more than others. Presumably the tendency to seek cognitive simplification leads to the adoption of heuristics which are inconsistent with our individual benefit-cost approach.[12] Instead several descriptive rules of behavioral decision making are thought to be better.

The representativeness rule leads people to base probability estimates on similarity even when prior odds are different. For example, a physician diagnoses that a patient has a disease based on the similarity of the symptoms to the textbook stereotype and ignores other known relevant information about the patient. The availability rule leads people to base probability estimates on how readily the situation can be brought to mind even when ease is misleading. Probabilities are based on the frequency of hearing about an event rather than actual frequencies. Thus news coverage would lead people to overestimate the probability of nuclear fatalities and underestimate the probability of death from asthma. Finally the anchoring rule leads people to choose a reference point and make adjustments from it slowly. This gradual adjustment can cause people to be unduly conservative and underweigh new information.[13]

Of the evidence in support of the behavioral, descriptive rules two studies are notable. Howard Kunreuther posits a sequential model of decision making in which the loss, even if catastrophic, is ignored if it is below some threshold level. He studied consumer response to highly subsidized flood insurance and found that few bought flood insurance contrary to his estimates of positive individual net benefits. He concluded that people have great difficulty and make mistakes when processing information on low probability, high loss events.[14] A fatal traffic accident can be considered such an event. The other study by David Grether and Charles Plott analyzes experimental gambling behavior. Different situations are concocted to present the same bet to people. Contrary to an expected net benefit model they find that people change their preferences depending on whether the choices are considered at the same time or assessed separately. In other words, they find that people reverse their preferences if a bet is framed differently.[15] The policy implication which might be interpreted is centralized decision making on traffic safety might be better than faulty individual decisions. Mandatory air bags, for example, might compensate for the suspected individual tendency to ignore or be confused by risks of traffic fatalities.

Evidence of Competence

The results of the behavioral studies should not be considered in isolation but rather they should be compared to the evidence which indicates individuals are competent—even in the face of risks. With the experimental gambling study we should compare M. M. Ali's analysis of betting behavior at horse races. He finds that there is no significant difference between the returns of the daily double and a parley bet in which the winners of the first race bet their winnings on the second race. The identical return on two identical bets found in two different contexts is consistent with the expected utility, individual benefit cost model. Preferences were not reversed.[16] With the study of flood insurance we should compare the analysis of earthquake risks by David Brookshire and his colleagues. They find homeowners do respond to severe, earthquake hazards even though they are low probability, high loss events. Their analysis of California property values reveals that values are lower in areas with higher expected losses. Furthermore, the differences in property values correspond closely to experts' estimates of expected earthquake damages. Also, the estimates of expected damages are close to the average stated willingness to pay for houses with lower expected damages. This survey evidence is consistent with the housing market evidence; individuals are processing risk information competently.[17]

Research also exists which addresses directly the proposition of behavioral decision theory that bounded rationality leads people to use heuristics which in turn cause systematic error in traffic safety decisions. Max Hammerton and his colleagues specifically investigate the seriousness of bounds when people are asked to deal with traffic safety. They performed psychological laboratory experiments presenting situations which tested for willingness to deal with traffic risks, ability to rank traffic risks, accuracy of subjective risk relative to objective estimates of risk, and monetary valuation of reductions in traffic risks. The results show that people are willing and able to answer questions about traffic safety, there is no evidence of mendacity, people were coherent in that they were consistent in choices involving different bets and they were consistent over time. The Hammerton group reports that, as has been found in previous studies, people seem to be rather bad at ranking unfamiliar activities in terms of risk and that there is evidence of anchoring. They also find, however, that people are much better at ranking risks associated with transport modes. They conclude that, on balance, in familiar activities and situations such as those inherent in traffic safety decisions there is a basis for optimism concerning broad correspondence between subjective and objective probabilities.[18] We should take this correspondence as a general finding. A consistent underlying scale for frequency of lethal events exists even though the scale differs from that of the actual frequency for groups and individuals – error but not total incompetence.

The survey finding of general correspondence between subjective and objective risks is consistent with a wealth of observational data on automobile safety belt use. Surprisingly, given an apparent conventional wisdom that seat belt use is too low and that all people should always wear their belts, a wide variety of studies yield results which indicate that indeed people do respond, and respond appropriately, to situations with different benefits and costs of seat belt use.

Descriptive studies (which do not carefully isolate factors) report seat belt use which is consistent with our interpretation that vehicle occupants respond appropriately to perceived differences in benefits and costs. In their 1973 review of seat belt use G. Fhanér and M. Hane find that use is higher where belts are perceived effective and inconvenience and discomfort are low. A 1978 survey by NHTSA found that belt use was highest on western highways and interstates. Net benefits are greatest for such driving since speeds are the highest and trips are the longest.[19]

A more recent and thorough study of factors which affect seat belt use was completed for NHTSA in 1983. First, J.M.B. Mayas and colleagues reviewed approximately 200 previous studies and identified factors which are consistently found to influence safety belt use. A profile of driver and situation for use of seat belts would be: a well-educated, higher socioeconomic status, married person who drives a smaller, foreign car on the highway for longer distances at higher speeds. Since the profile is based on pairwise comparisons of belt use of each factor, they would include urban dweller of a newer car, but these factors are highly correlated with those already mentioned. Second, they performed their own study of 197 Maryland drivers whom they observed and later interviewed face to face and 1,020 people who reside all over the nation and whom they interviewed by telephone. Their analysis confirmed the profile gleaned from the literature and added new information. Drivers of foreign cars and cars with combined lap and shoulder belts use belts more because of greater comfort and convenience. Drivers use belts more in poor weather and drivers with a young child in the family are found to be more likely to increase their belt use. Well educated, high status drivers who are married with young children have high values of safety. people who travel in small cars at higher speeds in bad weather perceive safety productivity of belts. People take long trips in foreign cars with comfortable lap and shoulder belts have low use costs.[20]

Results from the 1983 Nationwide Personal Transportation Study (NPTS) are again consistent with our individual net benefit model. Based on a survey of over 13,000 drivers, my calculations of NPTS data show people use belts more on wet, snowy or icy roads, than under clear road conditions and more on long trips than on short trips.[21]

A pilot study of shoulder belt usage is nearly unique because it isolates a benefit change. A survey of belt use was done on a trip from Baltimore to Pittsburgh on Labor Day 1981. During the trip a severe thunderstorm was encountered, which raised the perceived risk of accidental injury. Of the 125 drivers observed only 13 percent wore belts before the storm, but after the storm use more than doubled.

Another study of drivers of small cars and large cars also isolates a perceived benefit difference — the size of car. Over 2,500 observations were collected through photographs and matched with Michigan vehicle registration and driver license information. analysis showed that drivers of small cars partly compensate for the inherently greater risk they face and that one way they compensate is to use seat belts more. Statistical control for driver age contributes to the strong result. Since younger drivers who take more risks tend to drive smaller cars, simple correlations used in some studies have been misleading. Both the storm and car size studies isolate the effect of a benefit factor holding other factors constant. Both studies isolate factors to measure single rather than joint effects of factors which influence belt use.[22]

Multivariate analysis of belt use isolate the separate effects of several individual variables at the same time. In my own work I employ an individual benefit-cost approach and multivariate probit analysis to explain voluntary seat belt use and nonuse. For a national sample of over 1,800 drivers in 1972 I find that the probability of use is higher the greater are the expected net private benefits of belt use.

Usage is greater for drivers for whom:

- the intrinsic safety productivity of belts is the greatest,

- the value of injury avoidance is greatest, and
- the costs of using belts are lowest.[23]

Two recent multivariate studies support these earlier findings. For a national sample of over 2,000 drivers in 1983 Patrick McCarthy does a logit analysis of belt use, giving particular attention to travel conditions under which trips are made. He finds drivers in risky environments are more likely to use their seat belts. Through logit analysis of his own 1984 survey of drivers in two eastern cities Clifford Winston finds that belt use varies systematically with perceived benefits and costs. His results show drivers are particularly sensitive to the time it takes to fasten seat belts.[24]

The seat belt use evidence gives a clear indication of how useful our individual net benefit approach is for understanding traffic safety behavior. Studies of usage show that sufficient incentive, information and competency exists for different people in different travel situations to use seat belts differently in accordance with their own evaluation of the net benefits.

TRAFFIC SAFETY PROBLEMS: A MATTER OF DEGREE

An individual benefit-cost framework allows us to think about traffic safety behavior and re-examine the original mandate for policy as contained in the Vehicle Safety and Highway Safety Acts. Human response and appropriate policy are quite different depending on the approach taken. A technological approach, which was the basis for the Vehicle Safety Act, rules out human response and focuses on increases in vehicle crashworthiness. A risk homeostatic approach focuses on human response which tends to offset imposed technological changes. Our general framework focuses on individual choices by which target levels of safety can be increased by design changes and by which imposed design changes can be offset to the extent the target level of safety is not possibly increased. The human response depends on the individual's valuation of the benefits and costs. As long as current individual safety decisions are good, then no further policy action is appropriate. The decisions of individual travelers already reflect the advantages and disadvantages of traffic safety activity.

An Assessment of the Evidence

A traffic safety problem arises for society if travelers fail to make good decisions. Sufficient incentive, information and competence must exist for individual decisions to be good social safety decisions. A fruitful way to view the decisions is as a matter of degree. External effects of individual actions exist, but they appear small relative to the effects on the individuals themselves. External financial effects have been exaggerated by confusing total benefits or total costs with benefits or costs beyond the individual. Perhaps information inadequacy would be a problem in another time and place, but considerable information is available today in the United States from individual, commercial and public sources. A comparison to a world without such information is irrelevant. Although improvement is always possible current incentives and information are adequate for reasonably good traffic safety decisions overall.

Regardless of incentives and information, travelers must be sufficiently competent to make good decisions. The belief that individuals are incompetent to make risky decisions arises from research on behavioral decision rules in complex situations and on attitudes. Traffic safety decisions are suspect because risks may be misperceived and expected safety benefits may be undervalued. Ola Svenson and his colleagues, for example, report based on their attitudinal study that subjects show optimism bias; they feel they are more skillful and safer than typical drivers. They state that drivers who feel immune may discount measures such as seat belts.[25] A summary of this and other representative evidence of representative incompetence is presented in column 2 of Table 2-1. Next to these results, in column 3, is the evidence of competence for each subject: natural hazards and insurance, gambling, risk perception, and safety belt use.

Overall, we would be hard pressed to weigh this evidence and dismiss individual decision makers as incompetent. On the contrary, if we place the greatest weight on traffic safety and not natural hazards, gambling or risk perception, and on analysis of activity such as safety belt use and not attitudes, then we can see that travelers are not incompetent. They respond to various traffic risks by taking action which they see as being beneficial and worth it. Clearly competency is a matter of degree. Individual traffic safety decisions are not made by perfectly altruistic, all-knowing and infallibly calculating roadway users. Neither are they made by people who are totally unmotivated, ignorant and incompetent. Should bounded rationality be a relevant phenomenon, it would not imply unbounded incompetency. Considerable competency exists.

My first conclusion is that the individual benefit-cost approach is highly useful for understanding traffic safety behavior and for thinking about traffic safety policy. The framework is general enough to incorporate the technological and risk homeostatic approaches as special cases. My second conclusion is that roadway users are sufficiently competent and their safety

Table 2-1   REPRESENTATIVE EVIDENCE ON THE INDIVIDUAL BENEFIT-COST APPROACH [a]

Subject	Evidence of Incompetence	Evidence of Competence
Natural Hazards and Insurance	Homeowners fail to purchase subsidized flood insurance because they ignore low probability events; Kunreuther	Homeowners perceive earthquake risks and lower property values and stated willingness to pay equal earthquake damage; Brookshire et al.
Gambling	Bettors in gambling experiments reverse their preference if the same bet is framed differently; Grether and Plott	Racetrack bettors correctly treat the daily double and a parley bet as the same bet, despite different context; Ali
Risk Perception	Experimental results indicate people's subjective risk estimates differ from objective estimates; Slovic and Fischhoff	Survey results indicate that people are good at ranking risks associated with traffic; Hammerton et al.
Safety Belt Use	Experimental results of attitudinal research indicates drivers think they are more skillful and safer than average; Svenson et al.	Analysis of belt usage shows that differences in use correspond to differences in benefits and costs to individual drivers; Blomquist and Mayas et al.

[a] Studies referred to in this table are cited in the text.

decisions sufficiently good that the burden of proof is on proposers of additional, aggressive safety measures. The burden is to demonstrate that the expected, safety result expected after the measure is implemented is worth it and superior to that reached by individual travelers. The burden is to show the superiority in a context which recognizes human response and which recognizes individual costs. The claimed social desirability of mandated devices (perhaps air bags) is overstated because driver competency and the quality of individual safety decisions is underestimated.

An Assessment of Demands for More Aggressive Safety Policy

My assessment is that the traditional types of potential failure due to insufficient incentives and information and the new type of potential failure due to incompetency in processing risks are not compelling reasons for pursuing an aggressive safety policy beyond our basic traffic laws and public safety activity. The impetus for aggressive policy measures proposed by some advocates of strict injury control seems to have another basis, paternalism.[26] Paternalism can be based on a judgment that those people making the decisions are not sufficiently good enough to make the decisions themselves and that others will do better. A traditional parental duty is to substitute adult judgment for their own children's judgment as appropriate within a family. Melvin Bergheim aside, the paternalistic demand for safety policy which substitutes centralized decision making for individual adult decision making is indeed fundamentally different philosophically. Given the evidence which shows substantial individual competence in traffic safety decisions we can understand why questions are raised about safety regulations and why paternalism is controversial. Contrast Bergheim's philosophy with that of a noted Presbyterian minister, Bruce Larson. Larson urges people to consider creative risk taking and states that he is convinced that an inordinate need for safety is actually a form of mental illness.[27] His assertion that minimizing the risk of traffic accident injury actually may turn out to be unhealthy is bold, but it is actually compatible with a general approach to individual decision making. Clearly it is incompatible with a narrow goal of improving traffic safety as much as possible. Individual decision making surely is imperfect and the social traffic problem does exist, but for each it is a matter of degree. The traffic safety mandate places emphasis on total fatality and accident figures and hence exaggerates the severity of any safety problem. Our net benefit approach focuses on socially efficient individual decisions by roadway users, how policy measures will improve individual decisions, and the goal of an appropriate balance between traffic safety and other competing individual and social concerns. The assessment that existing incentives, information and competence are sufficient for individual decisions to produce reasonably good social safety decisions means that the general analytical justification for additional aggressive safety measures is weak. Because the analytical basis is weak the demand for additional safety measures becomes essentially parental or philosophical. In this context we should not be surprised that policy which attempts to impose a risk free traffic environment becomes a controversial issue.

Traffic Safety Policy

Notwithstanding controversy, analysis of traffic safety activity should and will be done. Our individual net benefit approach is a useful framework for thinking about traffic safety policy. In the design stage the framework allows us to consider the entire safety system which includes technology, travel environment and human behavior. The interaction among these elements must be estimated and incorporated in order to avoid costly policy mistakes. The interaction may also be crucial to successful implementation of policy measures. The framework is useful because it facilitates the paramount comparison between decisions based on individual net benefits and outcomes from imperfect implementation of imperfect policy. Finally at the evaluation stage the framework is useful because it facilitates accurate estimation of the effects of policy on the entire safety system including interaction between travelers and their safety environment. Quality policy evaluation is essential to the reformulation of existing imperfect policy and to improving the formulation of future policy.

NOTES

[1] U. S. Congress. House of Representatives. Committee on Interstate and Foreign Commerce. *Traffic Safety.* Hearings. 89th Congress, 2nd Session, Part 1, 1966, p. 538.

[2] For Haddon's testimony concerning the technological approach see U. S. Congress. Senate. Committee on Government Operations. *Federal Role in Traffic Safety.* Hearings before a subcommittee on Executive Reorganization. 89th Congress, 1st Session, 1965, Part 1 and Part 2. The National Traffic Safety Agency and the National Highway Safety Agency evolved into what in 1970 became the National Highway Traffic Safety Administration.

[3] According to the technological approach safety policy benefits (B) would be:

$$B = \sum_{k=1}^{m} \sum_{i=1}^{n} [\Delta P_r (I_k / A_i)] P_r (A_i)$$

where $\sum$ is summation, Δ is change in, P_r is probability of. And where there are m types of injuries (I) including fatal, and n types of accidents (A). The assumption is that $Pr(A_i)$ is constant.

[4] Wilde's approach explains how roadway users react to changes in the traffic environment. For an elaboration of his psychological approach see Gerald J. S. Wilde. "The Theory of Risk Homeostasis: Implications for Safety and Health." *Risk Analysis* 2, 4 (1982): 209–225.

[5] The risk homeostatic approach implies that safety policy can increase traffic safety through insurance rates, traffic fines, driver education and other measures which influence the benefits and costs of safety as perceived by roadway users. For detail on such incentive systems see Gerald J. S. Wilde and Paul A. Murdoch. "Incentive Systems for Accident-Free and Violation-Free Driving in the General Population." *Ergonomics* 25, 10 (1982): 879–890.

[6] A brief, mathematical exposition of the approach to traffic safety based on individual benefits and costs is given in the appendix.

[7] For a review of recent estimates of values of risk reduction see Glenn Blomquist "Estimating the Value of Life and Safety: Recent Developments" in M. W. Jones-Lee, ed., *The Value of Life and Safety* (New York: North Holland, 1982).

[8] The financial externalities for mortality risks are estimated in Martin J. Bailey *Reducing the Risks to Life: Measurement of the Benefits* (Washington, D.C.: American Enterprise Institute, 1980). My calculation is based on figures found in U. S. Department of Transportation. National Highway Traffic Safety Administration. *The Economic Cost to Society of Motor Vehicle Accidents.* DOT HS 806 342, January 1983, pp. I-4 and I-5.

[9] Total costs of motor vehicle accidents are sometimes presented as a measure of need for more traffic safety policy action. For example, see Nelson S. Hartunian, Charles N. Smart and Mark S. Thompson *The Incidence and Economic Costs of Major Health Impairments* (Lexington, Mass.: Lexington Books, 1981). According to our general framework for thinking about traffic safety the correct measure is the smaller, external costs.

[10] Controversy surrounds *The Car Book* because of the simplistic approach that is used to represent crashworthiness and questionable judgment. The standard requires that cars pass tests for 30 mph crashes, but the results in *The Car Book* are based on 35 mph crashes. Only six of the cars tested passed all the tests. Consumers wonder why NHTSA is interested in 35 mph crashes if the 30 mph standard is a good one—a result of the safe-unsafe technological approach. Manufacturers cry foul and wonder why the rules of the game have been changed ex post. The information rationale for *The Car Book* is clear and defensible, the implementation of the idea is somewhat questionable.

[11] A summary and interpretation of the evidence is found in the criticism of risk homeostasis by Paul Slovic and Baruch Fischhoff "Targeting Risks" *Risk Analysis* 2, 4 (1982): 227–234. Nearly all social scientists study human behavior; of course, "Behavioral" describes a particular psychological approach which differs from others such as social learning theory. Behavioral appears to be a school of thought in psychology just as monetarist describes a school of thought in economics.

[12] See Herbert A. Simon "A Behavioral Model of Rational Choice" *Quarterly Journal of Economics* 69 (February 1955): 174–183.

[13] For a more detailed presentation of these descriptive models see Paul J. Shoemaker "The Expected Utility Model: Its Variants, Purposes, Evidence and Limitations" *Journal of Economic Literature* 20 (June 1982) especially pages 551–552.

[14] See Howard Kunreuther "Limited Knowledge and Insurance Protection" *Public Policy* 24 (Spring 1976): 227–261. When this result is combined with a view that drivers act as if they think they are exceptionally skilled at accident avoidance lead some to conclude that individuals are bad decision makers. For example, see B. Fischhoff "Cognitive Liabilities and Product Liability" *Journal of Products Liability* 1 (1977): 207–220.

[15] See David M. Grether and Charles R. Plott. "Economic Theory of Choice and the Preference Reversal Phenomenon." *American Economic Review* 69 (September 1979): 623–638.

[16] See Mukhtar M. Ali "Probability and Utility Estimates for Racetrack Bettors" *Journal of Political Economy* 85 (August 1977): 803–816.

[17] See David S. Brookshire, Mark A. Thayer, John Tschirhart and William D. Schulze "A Test of the Expected Utility Model: Evidence from Earthquake Risks" *Journal of Political Economy* 93 (April 1985): 369–389.

[18] See M. Hammerton, M. W. Jones-Lee and V. Abbott "The Consistency and Coherence of Attitudes to Physical Risk: Some Empirical Evidence" *Journal of Transport Economics and Policy* 16 (May 1982): 181–200 and especially page 192.

[19] See G. Fhanér and M. Hane "Seat Belts: Factors Influencing Their Use: A Literature Survey" *Accident Analysis and Prevention* 5 (1973): 27–43 and U.S. Department of Transportation. National Highway Traffic Safety Administration. *Safety Belt Usage: Survey of the Traffic Population.* DOT HS 803 354. January 1978.

[20] See J. M. B. Mayas, N. K. Boyd, M. A. Collins and B. I. Harris. *A Study of Demographic, Situational, and Motivational Factors Affecting Restraint Usage in Automobiles.* Report for National Highway Traffic Safety Administration. DOT HS-806 402. February 1983 especially pages 14–15 and 112–114.

[21] See Glenn C. Blomquist "Motorist Use of Safety Equipment." A paper presented at the American Economic Association meeting held in Chicago, Illinois on December 28–30, 1987.

[22] The storm study is found in John D. Graham, Max Henrion and Granger M. Morgan. "An Analysis of Federal Policy Toward Automobile Safety Belts and Air Bags." Working Paper, Department of Engineering and Public Policy and School of Public Affairs, Carnegie-Mellon University, November 1981 on pages 16-17. The car size study is Paul Wasielewski and Leonard Evans "Do Drivers of Small Cars Take Less Risk in Everyday Driving?" *Risk Analysis* 5, 1 (1985): 25–32.

[23] The study differs from descriptive studies in that the model guides the choice of variables and in that the multivariate analysis isolates the effect of each factor holding other factors constant. See Glenn Blomquist "Economics of Safety and Seat Belt Use" *Journal of Safety Research* 9 (December 1977): 179–189.

[24] These two studies are by Patrick S. McCarthy "Seat Belt Usage Rates: A Test of Peltzman's Hypothesis" *Accident Analysis and Prevention* 18 (October 1986): 425–438 and Clifford Winston and Associates *Blind Intersection: Policy and the Automobile Industry* (Washington, D.C.: Brookings Institution, 1987). For preliminary multilogit analysis results of the 1983 NPTS data, see Blomquist "Motorist Use of Safety Equipment."

[25] The study referred to is: Ola Svenson, Baruch Fischhoff and Donald MacGregor "Perceived Driving Safety and Seatbelt Usage" *Accident Analysis and Prevention* 17 (April 1985): 119–134.

[26] For a lively exchange which illustrates the clash between people with different philosophies see Richard J. Perkins "Perspective on the Public Good" *American Journal of Public Health* 71 (March 1981): 294–295 and Susan P. Baker and Stephen P. Teret "Freedom and Protection: A Balancing of Interests" American Journal of Public Health 71 (March 1981): 295–297.

A rationale for a government traffic safety policy which is distinct from incentives, information, incompetency and paternalism is the idea that a transfer of wealth (in the form of more crashworthy vehicles) can be from auto manufacturers to consumers. In the 1965 traffic safety hearing Senator Ribicoff reasoned that since Detroit makes a lot of money it should use profits for safety and Senator Robert Kennedy chastised the executives of General Motors for making $1,700 million in profit and only spending a bit over $1 million on safety (U. S. Congress, Senate, *Traffic Safety*, Parts 1 and 2, 1965, pp. 241 and 784). This notion that companies, not consumers and taxpayers, pay for any safety gains undoubtedly explains some of the enthusiasm for traffic safety policy and especially FMVSS's. This is wishful thinking because costs are much more likely to be borne ultimately by consumers than by managers and stockholders. The reason is that since firms can adjust to the regulation the easily—identified, initial incidence can be quite different from the final economic incidence. A complete distributional analysis may well reflect that some deserving groups such as low income consumers are actually worse off with the policy. The 1973 Mattress Flammability Standard set by the Consumer Product Safety Commission resulted in income redistributions from the low income to high income families and from small to large producers. See Peter Linneman "The Effects of Consumer Safety Standards: The 1973 Mattress Flammability Standard." *Journal of Law and Economics* 23 (October 1980): 461–480.

[27] See Bruce Larson: *There's a Lot More to Health Than Not Being Sick* (Waco, Texas: Word Books, 1981).

APPENDIX TO CHAPTER 2

A Mathmatical Exposition of the Individual Benefit-Cost Approach

As stated in Chapter 2 the focus of the individual benefit-cost approach is on the roadway user's choice of a target level of safety and choice of ways of achieving that safety. For expositional purposes the approach is couched in terms of motorist behavior and striking examples. The approach applies, however, to all roadway users and includes subtle responses which may occur over extended periods of time. The approach is general in that mandated technological changes and responses based on psychophysiological arousal are incorporated.[1]

A motorist will experience one of two states of the world; either an accident does not occur or an accident occurs over some period of time. The probability that a motorist is involved in an accident (p) is influenced by the driver's own safety effort (e) and government safety measures (s). The production function for accident risk is specified by $p(e,s)$ with $p_e < 0$, $p_{ee} > 0$, $p_s < 0$, $p_{ss} > 0$, and $p_{es} > 0$ where the signs of the first and second derivatives shown represent typical production conditions. For example $p_s < 0$ means that the partial effect of an increase in enforcement activity against drunk driving would reduce the probability of an accident. The loss which a motorist incurs in an accident (L) depends on the motorist's own safety effort and government safety measures also; $L(e,s)$ with $L_e < 0$, $L_{ee} > 0$, $L_s < 0$, $L_{ss} > 0$, and $L_{es} > 0$. The expected loss from an accident is determined by the probability of an accident as well as the size of the loss. Notice that the assumption $p_{es} > 0$ and $L_{es} > 0$ reflect the individual and government safety efforts are similar and are substitutes in production. Finally, let there be disutility (V) associated with driver safety effort; $V(e)$ with $V_e > 0$ and $V_{ee} > 0$.

Now, if the motorist has income (I) and is risk neutral, then expected utility is shown in Equation 1:

$$U = p(e,s)[I - V(e) - L(e,s)] + [1 - p(e,s)]$$
$$[1 - V(e)] \text{ or simply}$$
$$U = I - V(e) - p(e,s)L(e,s)$$

Equation 1 shows that expected utility equals the probability of an accident times the payoff if an accident occurs, plus the probability of no accident times the payoff if no accident occurs. More simply expected utility is income less disutility less the expected accident loss. In balancing the benefits and costs of safety effort the motorist increases effort through use of safety belts and moderate speeds or similar activity until $dU/de = 0$ or as shown in Equation 2:

$$-V_e = p_e L + p L_e$$

which implies the optimum level of motorist safety effort. The right amount of private safety effort for the individual motorist is the effort for which the marginal value of the utility cost just equals the marginal benefit of the reduction in expected loss. The reduction in loss can occur through a reduction in the probability (p) or the size of the loss (L). When aggregated over all drivers, the optimum safety efforts determine the aggregate number of fatalities and injuries.

The result indicates that factors such as vehicle safety are given considerable attention exclusive of regulation. The individual safety result also indicates that in general motorists will change their behavior (e) in response to a change in mandated safety (s). To determine the effect of a change in government safety effort on motorist safety effort treat equation 2 as an implicit function and find $^{de}/_{ds}$ as shown in Equation 3:

$$\frac{de}{ds} = -\frac{-p_{es} L - p_e L_s - p_s L_e - p L_{es}}{-V_{ee} - p_{ee} L - 2 p_e L_e - p L_{ee}} < 0$$

The second order condition for utility maximization is that $d^2U/d_e{}^2 < 0$, where $d^2U/d_e{}^2$ turns out to be equal to the denominator in equation 3. It follows that $^{de}/_{ds}$ is negative which means that an increase in government safety measures will induce motorists to decrease their own efforts. By symmetry it also follows that any exogenous change which increases the probability of an accident (p), say deteriorating highway conditions, will induce motorists to increase their own efforts. The model does not imply how large induced response will be, but the qualitative results are clear. Risk compensation (also known as behavioral feedback and offsetting behavior) is a normal human response in the context of a general framework for thinking about traffic safety.

NOTES TO APPENDIX

[1]The original model upon which this approach is based is Peltzman's model of driver behavior. See Sam Peltzman "The Effects of Automobile Safety Regulation." *Journal of Political Economy* 83 (August 1975): 677–726. Related models of worker safety and consumer product safety can be found in W. Kip Viscusi "The Impact of Occupational Safety and Health Regulation." *The Bell Journal of Economics* 10 (Spring 1979): 117–148 and "The Lulling Effect: The Impact of Child-Restraint Packaging on Aspirin and Analgesic Ingestions." *American Economic Review* 74 (May 1984): 324–327.

For a presentation with a slightly different emphasis than found in this approach, see Glenn Blomquist "A Utility Maximization Model of Driver Traffic Safety Behavior." *Accident Analysis and Prevention* 18 (October 1986): 371–375.

CHAPTER 3
THE CONTRIBUTION OF VEHICLE SAFETY STANDARDS TO TRAFFIC SAFETY

CHANGES IN TRAFFIC FATALITY RATES

According to the National Highway and Traffic Safety Administration's *Motor Vehicle Safety 1979* the contribution of national policy to traffic safety is substantial.

> The Federal safety standards and programs for highway and motor vehicle safety that have been instituted since 1966 have combined to reduce the fatality rate (number of deaths per 100 million vehicle miles driven) by 39 percent. In other words, a motorist today can drive more than 1,600 miles with the same degree of risk as someone who drove 1,000 miles in 1966. This improvement has come about despite large increases in traffic that could have sent the death rate higher—registered motor vehicles up 67 percent; licensed drivers up 42 percent; and vehicle miles driven up 65 percent.[1]

The message is clear: traffic safety policy has produced a sizable reduction in the risk of fatal accident despite the adverse effects of some demographic and economic trends.

Despite the clarity of the message it is not clear that it is correct. It is revealing to examine how it is figured that the standards and programs have reduced the fatality rate by 39 percent from 1966 to 1979. Simply calculate the percentage change in the actual fatality rate over the period; it is 39 percent.[2] The reasoning is whatever happens to the fatality rate is the result of traffic safety policy! A generous interpretation is that the claim reflects the difficulty in isolating the effect of safety regulation among the effects of various other effects which are unrelated to traffic safety policy. The absurdity of attributing all changes in the fatality rate, however, is easily illustrated.

Imagine a rather carefree fellow who spends most of his time consuming some of the finer things in life — such as tanning tournaments, radio talk shows, TV, and starring as wide receiver in games of football. Through no fault of his own this fellow is named National Traffic Safety Administrator and given the responsibility of reducing the nation's fatality rate. He is given no office space, no staff and no budget with which to carry out his duties. While making occasional appearances in the lobbies, cafeterias and washrooms around the nation's capital, this fellow continues his heavy commitment to carefree living. The remarkable thing is that in his annual report, oral of course, he claims that he has had a successful year because the fatality rate has declined. He amazes people by performing the same feat year after year with only one year off until he retires and is given a generous annuity for his 15 years of successful service.

Absurd? Yes, of course. But if the nation had been the U. S. and the period had been 1946 to 1961, it could have been true. As noted earlier, with no federal motor vehicle safety standards and only a few fragmented federal traffic safety programs the fatality rate declined each year from 1946 to 1961 except in 1950.[3] (The decline is shown in Figure 1-1.) Would our carefree fellow have been as successful in the 1970's? Some would argue "no" and some would argue "yes, almost." The point is that there must be some idea of what the fatality rate would have been without traffic safety policy, a counterfactual, in addition to the observable, actual rate in order to measure the contribution of policy to traffic safety. Just as it would be incorrect to blame traffic safety policy for all increases in the fatality rate, or other indicator, it is incorrect to credit traffic safety policy for all reductions. The appropriate measure of policy's contribution is difference between the observed fatality rate and the (higher) rates which would have resulted without the policy. The difference between the observed (lower) fatality rates and the (higher) rates which would have resulted without the policy is the appropriate measure whether the trend is upward or downward. The challenge is to estimate the fatality rates which would have been observed had there been no national traffic safety policy, the counterfactual estimates . Several studies have made such estimates and measured the impacts of standards on traffic safety. We review these studies in approximate chronological order.

EVIDENCE ON THE SAFETY EFFECTS

The Initial Technological Predictions

The rationale for federal motor vehicle safety standards is that mandated safety equipment will produce safety gains effectively. As discussed in Chapter 2 this technological approach focuses on increases in crash survivability and implicitly assumes that the frequency of crashes is unaffected. As long as the safety equipment improves crashworthiness the standards must increase safety according to this approach. The initial standards required the following major design changes:

- seat belt installation front and back,
- energy absorbing steering column,
- penetration resistant windshield,
- dual braking system, and
- padded instrument panel.

The intrinsic safety effect of this equipment was estimated through study of comparisons of actual crashes and through study of simulated crashes in laboratories.

Numerous such safety engineering studies were carried out and published in the period 1967 to 1972. According to the review of these studies by Sam Peltzman, most of the expected reduction in the occupant fatality rate was expected from lap seat belts (7 to 16 percent reduction) and energy absorbing steering columns (4 to 7 percent reduction). For all five of the major design changes the expected reduction in the 1972 occupant fatality rate was in the 10 to 25 percent range. The implied expected reduction in the 1972 total traffic fatality rate was in the 7 to 20 percent range. The consensus estimates were close to the larger effects.[4]

The technological production for years more recent than 1972 are greater. The growth is expected as older, unregulated cars are used less and as more standards take effect. Due in part to these factors and in part to different judgment the U. S. General Accounting Office reports an expected reduction in the occupant death rate in the 15 to 35 percent range.[5]

The Initial Evidence Based on Fatality Rates — Peltzman

Sam Peltzman's methodological approach differs from the technological approach in that he focuses on human behavior especially driver choice.[6] He begins with an individual benefit-cost framework to traffic safety and combines with it findings from other safety studies to construct counterfactual estimates of traffic fatality rates, hypothetical rates which would have occurred without a national traffic safety policy. We will examine his study in some detail because most of the studies are similar in crucial aspects and hence we can examine other studies more quickly. Peltzman's study is pivotal in that it was one of the first comprehensive evaluative studies. It reintroduced human behavior into traffic safety thinking.

Peltzman's model emphasizes driver choice between safety and other desirables such as work or leisure time and the varying benefits and costs of safety equipment in different driving situations. Peltzman uses this approach to analyze fatal accident rates as measured by traffic fatalities per 100 million vehicle miles of travel. The fatality rate is adjusted for changes in the urban-rural composition of driving and the share of travel on limited-access highways. In the econometric, time series analysis, the parameters of the multiple regression equation are estimated for the pre-regulatory period, 1947 to 1965, counterfactual fatality rates are projected for the period 1966 to 1972, and the contribution of traffic safety policy is discussed in terms of the differences. The regression results for total traffic fatalities for 1947 to 1965 are:

$$ATDR = \ -0.172P \ + 0.884Y \ + \ -0.074T \ + \ -.359A \ + \ 1.843S \ + \ -.827K$$
$$(-1.792) \qquad (4.317) \qquad (13.900) \quad (2.591) \quad (3.863) \quad (12.232)$$
$$R^2 = .994 \ D.W. = 2.080$$

> Where ATDR is the adjusted total death rate (per vehicle mile);
>
> P is an index of accident (dollar) costs based on physician and hospital costs and insurance premiums;
>
> Y is real labor (earned) income per working age adult;
>
> T is a time trend which represents permanent income perhaps and other secular changes;
>
> A is alcohol consumption as measured by per capita consumption of distilled spirits;
>
> S is average speed of motor vehicles on noninterstate rural roads at off-peak hours;
>
> K is the ratio of 15 to 25 year old population to the rest of the population; and

all variables except T are in logarithms.[7]
The variable T represents the pre-regulatory secular trend;
P and Y are driver behavior variables; and
A, S and K are known correlates although they may have
    economic interpretations.

The results indicate that before modern safety regulations there was a strong secular decline in the total traffic fatality rate and that rates were increased by travel time costs (Y), alcohol consumption (A), faster travel (S) and a younger population (K) and decreased private accident costs (P). From the estimated effect and the actual change the average annual short-run contribution of each variable is calculated. In terms of hypothetical one-percent increases in each factor, the most important variable is speed which causes a 1.8 percent increase in the fatality rate, followed by labor income which causes a 0.9 percent increase, and youth which causes a 0.8 percent increase. When these estimated effects are multiplied times the actual change in the variable for the entire period, vehicle speed is found to be the most important contributing factor, followed by income and youth. The total short-run contributions of all five factors to the average annual change in the fatality rate is 5.3 percent, but it is more than offset by the average annual effect of all long-run adjustments of -7.4 percent. The net result for the pre-regulatory period is an average annual change in the fatality rate of -1.9 percent.[8]

To illustrate the usefulness of the model for understanding movements in the fatality rate, the estimated fatality rate can be calculated by multiplying the elasticity times the actual change in the factor for each of the five factors. As Peltzman reports, the model performs well over the period with the difference between the estimated and actual fatality rates never exceeding 2 percent.[9] The results shed a bit of light on the alarm over the rise in fatality rates that Senator Ribicoff and others conveyed in the hearings leading to the Vehicle Safety Act of 1966. The most important factor in explaining the rise in the early 1960's is the change in the youth variable caused by the postwar "baby boom." Peltzman estimates that if the ratio of the 15–24 year olds to the rest of the population had not changed from 1960 to 1965, then the decline in the fatality rate would have continued and the rate would have been -1 percent.[10] The estimated rate of decline is slower than the decline for years prior to 1960, but it is lower than the average annual increase of 2 percent which actually occurred.

Using the same methodology Peltzman estimates the contributions of modern traffic safety policy to reductions in the fatality rate. Counterfactual fatality rates are projected for each year during the regulatory period from 1966 to 1972 and compared to the rates which actually occurred. The differences are less than 2 percent, except in 1972 when it is 4 percent. Since the importance (elasticity) of each factor is estimated in the pre-regulatory period, the projections into the period covered by safety regulations are based on the assumption that there were no regulations and as such give us an idea of what would have happened without the regulations. If the regulations have been effective, then actual fatality rates should be less than rates projected on the assumption of no regulations. The projections leave, however, little room for the reduction of 39 percent claimed by NHTSA. The decline in the fatality rate during the regulatory period can be explained by nonregulatory factors such as: a slowing in the rate of increase in youthful drivers, the secular trend and rising accident costs. Based on the evidence, Peltzman's conclusion is that modern traffic safety policy's contribution to the decline in the total fatality rate has been negligible.

Peltzman's pessimistic conclusion is explained by his finding two divergent effects of vehicle safety standards – a reduction in the occupant fatality rate and an increase in the fatality rate of those other than occupants of regulated vehicles – non-occupants. Peltzman finds that the occupant fatality rate is lower than projected for the regulatory period. Vehicle crashworthiness increased. However, the nonoccupant fatality rate is substantially higher than projected, and the increase in nonoccupant fatalities more than offsets the decrease in occupant fatalities. For 1972 the occupant fatality rate is 7 percent lower than the projected rate, but it is not as much lower (20 percent) as a technological approach would predict. For 1972 the nonoccupant fatality rate is 43 percent higher than projected and the total fatality rate is 5 percent higher than projected.[11]

The increased driving intensity (risk compensation) led to consuming approximately a third of the increased crashworthiness from the safety standards and to a dramatic increase in nonoccupant fatalities. Drivers consumed some of the mandated safety by driving with greater intensity, say, faster and having more accidents. The increase in the accident rate offset some of the improved crashworthiness so that the fatality rate for occupants failed to decline as much as crashworthiness improved. Moreover, the increase in the accident rate raised the fatality rate for nonoccupants so much that it offset the safety gains for occupants. Peltzman's conclusion that the contribution of modern safety policy to traffic safety is negligible can be understood in terms of substituting regulated safety for some unregulated safety which would have been produced anyway by individuals (market displacement) and substituting nonsafety goals for regulated crashworthiness (risk compensation).

Evidence Based on Accident Severity Rate — GAO

The U.S. General Accounting Office (GAO) did not do a national evaluation of the vehicle safety standards by analyzing the trend in the traffic fatality rate. Instead its technological approach focuses on any reduction in the probability of vehicle occupants being killed or seriously injured if the occupants are in regulated cars instead of unregulated cars, when they are involved in an accident.[12] The premise of this approach is that the vehicle safety standards can be evaluated by studying the frequency for different model-year cars of occupants being killed or seriously injured when involved in accidents. The frequency of accident occurrence is assumed to be unaffected by the vehicle safety standards and is not considered.

The study investigates the improved crashworthiness of passenger cars due to the standards through multiple regression analysis of approximately 2 million auto accidents in North Carolina and New York from 1966 to 1974. The variable explained, the dependent variable, is the percent of drivers in accidents who were killed or severely injured. Driver fatality and injury rates (per accident) are compared for different model years of passenger cars. Severity of injury to a driver involved in an accident is explained by model year (which determines the mandated safety equipment on the auto), speed, sobriety, vehicle weight, usage of seat belts as well as driver age, number of violations, weather conditions, road type and other similar variables. The conclusions are that the vehicle safety standards for 1966 to 1973 autos reduced by approximately 25 percent the percentage of drivers in accidents who were seriously or fatally injured compared to drivers in accidents in pre–1966 models. Most of the estimated reduction occurred in the 1966 to 1970 models with little, if any, improvement in the 1971 to 1973 models.[13] The major weakness of the study is no attempt is made to estimate the impacts on accident frequency or travelers other than occupants of passenger cars. These impacts are assumed to be zero in estimating the effect of safety standards on total traffic fatalities.

Rebuttal to Peltzman's Findings — Robertson and Joksch

In view of the unprecedented finding that vehicle safety standards contributed little if anything to reducing the total fatality rate, it is not surprising that Peltzman's research was criticized. Peltzman's use of an approach with human behavioral response included instead of the prevailing technological approach was thought to border on the preposterous. Interestingly no superior alternative approach was offered formally. Almost exclusively, criticism from public health researchers was directed at the empirical work. We turn to a sample of the criticisms and comments on them.

Leon Robertson criticizes the regression equation which Peltzman uses for making projections into the regulatory period. Robertson asserts that the prediction equation is not robust with respect to the choice of the pre-regulatory period and shows that if one reestimates the equation using the period 1947 to 1959 the revised model tends to underpredict fatality rates by larger amounts each year from 1960 to 1965. He does not defend his choice of 1959. Robertson concludes: "...projections based on the model using the same variables in these and succeeding years would be expected to diverge from actual rates in the absence of regulation. Since the model does not accurately project actual death rates prior to regulation it cannot be used to estimate the effects of regulation."[14] To exclude, however, the years immediately preceding regulation is to arbitrarily discard valuable information. For example the greater sensitivity to youth in Peltzman's equation is reasonable since Robertson's shorter period excludes the important influence of youth on 1960–65 fatality rates.

Motorcyclists are improperly classified according to Robertson.[15] To Robertson it is wrong to equate motorcyclists with pedestrians since riding is more dangerous than walking and since mandatory helmet use was implemented during the regulatory period. A semantic problem is caused by lumping cyclists and walkers/runners together. We are better off to refer to both types as nonoccupants. The reasoning is clear though and it is that motorcycle riders are not treated as vehicle occupants because the car safety standards do not apply to them. Also, with Peltzman's approach which includes driver behavior cyclists may be affected by auto safety standards in the same way (adversely) as pedestrians.

Robertson proceeds to offer a modified version of Peltzman's prediction equation in which the accident cost variable is dropped, the youth variable is changed from "share of the population which is young" to the "share of youthful drivers in fatal accidents", the fatality rate for occupants is multiplied by the proportion of fatal accidents which involved passenger cars and the nonoccupant rate was backed out from the adjusted total fatality rate. Using the modified equation Robertson finds that actual fatality rates during the regulatory period from 1966 to 1972 are well below projected rates and that the measured contribution of vehicle safety standards is quite compatible with earlier technological analysis.[16] However, as Peltzman points out that each of the "corrections" made by Robertson is a matter of choice and that each is inconsistent with Peltzman's approach based on driver behavior. The regression equation is now misspecified.[17]

H. C. Joksch criticizes Peltzman's finding citing some of the same reasons given by Robertson and some new reasons. One argument is that Peltzman includes the wrong variables in the regression equation. This mistake leads to faulty projections into the regulatory period and, along with multicolinearity, to biased coefficients for the accident factors. Joksch states: "Peltzman does not empirically substantiate his assumption that the accident cost influences driver behavior."[18] That accident cost induces driver care in an implication of Peltzman's theory of driver behavior, not an assumption, and to omit it is to open the door to just the omitted variable bias Joksch suggests. In spite of any shortcomings in the accident cost variable described by Joksch, there is an indication that the accident cost should not be excluded in that it has the expected negative effect and is nearly statistically significant at the 10 percent level for a 1-tail test. Joksch suggests that Peltzman uses the wrong income variable (real earned income per adult of working age), that something like the Federal Reserve Board (FRB) Index of Industrial Products is better, and concludes that until it has been shown that Peltzman's income variable has a significantly better regression coefficient than one of the other income variables mentioned, Peltzman's arguments interpreting his income measure are unfounded. But Peltzman's uses an income variable appropriate for his approach which includes driver behavior.[19]

The striking characteristic of the preceding rebuttal to Peltzman's findings is that it appears to be ad hoc. No alternative framework to Peltzman's approach is offered explicitly. Robertson and Joksch, through their association with the Insurance Institute for Highway Safety and other organizations interested in highway safety, have become familiar with "known correlates" with fatal accidents and in that sense are clearly experts on some aspects of traffic accidents. Nonetheless, a reader of Carl Hempel on the virtue of good methodology in understanding complex phenomena or Glenn Snelbecker on the dangers of ad hoc approaches can evaluate the Peltzman and Robertson-Joksch exchange rather easily.[20] The attempted rebuttals serve to remind us that data can be analyzed an unlimited number of ways with quite different results. Without a methodological approach to guide the choice of relevant variable and to interpret the results (whatever they may be) we are left with ad hoc empiricism.

Evidence Based on Crash Involvements Rates — Robertson and Orr

Another more recent study by Robertson investigates the effectiveness of vehicle safety standards by analyzing 1975–1978 data on fatal accidents from the Fatal Accident Reporting System (FARS) for 236,205 vehicles.[21] Whereas the 1976 GAO study analyzed the fatality rate per accident, Robertson estimates and analyzes fatality rates per 100 million vehicle miles for each model year of car. This rate is called the total fatal crash involvement rate. The FARS data on fatalities by model year is combined with data on the number of vehicles registered by model year and with data on the number of miles driven by model year (for 1977 and adjusted by total mileage for the other years) to estimate the fatalities per vehicle mile traveled for each model year. Robertson calculates 120 fatal crash involvement rates (15 model years x 4 calendar years x 2 vehicle type — cars and trucks); the rate becomes the dependent variable in his multiple regression analysis. Implicitly following a technological approach to traffic safety, the fatal crash involvement rate is explained by whether or not the model year is covered by state and GSA regulations (1964 to 1977 models), whether or not the model year is covered by federal regulations (1968 to 1977 models), whether or not the vehicle is a car or truck, and vehicle age (age, age^2 and age^3). Vehicle type and vehicle age are included in the regression because they are, according to Robertson, "known correlates". No other reason is given for including these variables and excluding others. The regression estimates show a highly significant negative coefficient for federal regulation.

Robertson addresses the effect of vehicle safety standards on nonoccupants using the same approach he used to estimate the effect on occupants. From FARS data and other sources he calculates a pedestrian fatal crash involvement rate for each vehicle model year. The rate is calculated by dividing the number of pedestrians killed in an accident with a vehicle of a specified model year by the estimated number of miles driven in that model year of vehicle. Similar multiple regression analyses are applied to fatalities of motorcyclists and pedalcyclists who are separate from pedestrians. Finally, a total fatality crash involvement rate is calculated and analyzed using the same specification for regression analysis. Robertson finds that qualitatively nonoccupants are affected the same as occupants. Based on the estimated equations for the four fatal crash involvement rates, Robertson concludes that during the period 1975 to 1978 due to the vehicle safety standards 37,000 people were saved from traffic deaths — 26,500 occupants; 7,600 pedestrians; 1,000 pedalcyclists and 2,000 motorcyclists.[22]

Robertson appears to have found strong evidence that the safety standards did not increase nonoccupant risk and even made nonoccupants safer. One wonders if the evidence is not, in a sense, too strong.[23] The vehicle safety standards emphasize improved crashworthiness to protect occupants—the 200 series of FMVSS. Surprisingly, Robertson finds fatality reductions for nonoccupants which relatively are at least as strong as for occupants in terms of total fatalities within each group. If one uses fatality data for the years 1975 through 1978 and calculates the share of fatalities avoided in each group the relative reductions are: occupant fatalities are 16 percent less than they would have been had all vehicles been unregulated, pedestrian fatalities are 20 percent less, motorcyclist fatalities are 12 percent less, and pedalcyclist fatalities are 21 percent less. Perhaps the 100-series vehicle safety standards designed to enhance crash avoidance and FMVSS No. 211 designed to eliminate the Ben Hur effect of hub cap spinners have had a relatively larger safety effect on pedestrians (20 percent reduction) and pedalcyclists (21 percent reduction) than all of the vehicle safety standards including crashworthiness and crash avoidance have had on occupants (16 percent reduction), but it is a surprise.

The surprising results found by Robertson have been examined more closely by Lloyd Orr. Orr reanalyzes the same FARS data using the technological approach implicit in Robertson's research.[24] The difference is Orr does not accept Robertson's use of truck rates and the car-truck dummy variable in the regressions. He gives two reasons:

- safety regulations were for automobiles, not trucks, and

- the car-truck dummy variable is quite collinear with the regulation variables.

By construction the positive correlation between the car-truck dummy and the federal regulation dummy is .63 and between the same dummy and the state-GSA regulatory dummy is .85. When the regression for fatal crash involvement is estimated for cars only, the estimated safety effect of regulation decreases markedly. The safety effects for occupants, pedestrians and bicyclists are smaller and the estimate for motorcyclists indicates they are harmed. The revised estimate of lives saved is only 13 percent of Robertson's estimate. Orr also investigates different age specifications due to the high correlations between the age variables and the regulatory dummies (-.62 to -.85). If the age is entered in its linear form and the adverse estimated effect of the state-GSA dummy is considered, Orr demonstrates that the total safety effect is probably close to zero. Orr's changes to Robertson's analysis appear to be reasonable improvements. They are made in the spirit of a technological approach with statistical care. They demonstrate the sensitivity of Robertson's results and cause us to revise downward our beliefs about the safety effect. We should be careful to put much emphasis on either of these estimates because of the lack of an explicit approach which allows us to interpret the results.

Recent Evidence Based on Fatality Rate Analysis – Seven Studies

Oscar Cantu updates Peltzman's study by analyzing traffic fatality rates from 1947 to 1977, adding five years to the regulatory period.[25] Besides analyzing a longer and more recent period, he pursues several suggestions made by Robertson (in conversations) while at the same time maintaining the integrity of the regression model with respect to the household safety market approach. Cantu reconstructs Peltzman's data set, but makes some changes. He does not make the urban-rural mix adjustments to fatality rates (because he finds it confusing and perhaps arbitrary. He does not elaborate). In addition to analyzing the total fatality rate based on miles traveled by all vehicles he calculates fatality rates based on passenger car miles driven. He uses a better variable for alcohol, alcoholic content of beverage consumption per capita of the drinking age population. Additionally he uses a measure of the extent of regulation, the percentage of the car stock of 1964 and later vintage, and a qualitative (0–1) variable for the energy crunch which began in 1974.

Cantu's results on the contributions of the accident factors (accident cost, income, speed, alcohol, youth and the trend) are essentially the same as Peltzman's. For the total fatality rate based on all vehicle miles (which is the closer of the two to Peltzman's rate) Cantu finds a small but statistically significant effect of safety regulation on the total fatality rate. In 1977, for example, the reduction in the total fatality rate due to regulation is estimated to be 0.2 percent. The effect of the vehicle safety standards on nonoccupants is to increase their fatality rate significantly and even greater as Peltzman found. For his own definition of the fatality rates which are based on miles for regulated vehicles only Cantu's results are: that regulation contributed a small (but statistically insignificant) reduction to the fatality rate for auto occupants, that regulation led to a fairly large and statistically significant increase in the fatality rate for nonoccupants, and that the net contribution to the total fatality rate is small. Cantu's update of Peltzman's study leaves unchanged the finding that modern traffic policy's contribution is to the total traffic fatality rate negligible.

John Graham and Steven Garber critique what they refer to as the major previous study (Peltzman's) and offer an alternative analysis based on an updated data set with a variable which measures the extent of regulation.[26] In their critique they demonstrate that Peltzman's model yields estimates of positive overall safety effects if the functional form is linear rather than logarithmic. They point out that a form without the interactions implied by the multiplicative form may be just as plausible theoretically. What they do not discuss is any decrease in statistical fit (worse likelihood value) they incur when they switch functional forms.

Graham and Garber's primary contribution is to use an individual net benefit approach as did Peltzman and through regression analysis to estimate the effects of vehicle safety standards on traffic fatality rates. Regulation is measured by the proportion of miles driven in regulated cars. Some variables such as that for alcohol consumption are defined differently to try to reduce measurement error. Some variables such as small car travel are added to try to hold more constant traffic conditions other than regulation. The period of analysis is extended so that the years 1947 to 1980 are included. Three separate equations are estimated for vehicle (car, bus and truck) occupants, pedestrian and motorcyclists with appropriate changes for the nonoccupants. They find:

- occupant deaths are lowered by regulation — by as much as 17 to 29 percent,
- pedestrian deaths are not much affected — no statistical significance, and
- motorcyclist deaths are raised — by as much as 55 to 84 percent.

(Although they dismiss the affect on motorcyclists, the regulation coefficient is significant at the .05 level for a one-tail test in the first specification.)

Graham and Garber state that their findings imply that in 1980 11,000 to 20,000 occupant deaths were avoided by regulation. My calculation based on a 23 (midpoint) percent reduction in occupant deaths and a 70 percent increase in motorcyclist deaths is that total lives saved is approximately 8,500. Their figures are too high because they applied the regulatory effect to total deaths, not occupant deaths, and they ignored the adverse effect on motorcyclists.

John Graham uses the same regulation variable technique in another related study which covers the period 1947 to 1981.[27] He estimates the reduced form equation for a model in which fatality rate and speed are determined simultaneously. In practical terms, the only new variable is a dummy variable for the 55 m.p.h. speed limit. Curiously the price of gas is ignored despite theory and evidence that it is a determinant of speed.[28] This misspecification may explain the large size (39 percent for 1981) of the estimated reduction in the occupant fatality rate. He finds some weak evidence that nonoccupants are made less safe in that the (insignificant) regulation coefficient in the pedestrian equation is positive. He did not analyze motorcyclist and bicyclist deaths which are expected to be affected more than pedestrian deaths.

Robert Crandall uses the regulation variable technique for the same period, 1947 to 1981, but measures regulation by the proportion of miles driven by regulated cars weighted by existing estimates of improvements in crashworthiness.[29] While Crandall proports to use the simultaneous systems model he shares with Graham he chooses to explain fatalities, not fatality rates. His estimates imply a tremendous (unbelievable?) increase in safety for occupants and a decrease in safety for pedestrians and bicyclists. The estimated reduction in occupant deaths, 54 percent, is greater than the estimates of the most optimistic technological studies. The estimated decline in nonoccupant safety is based on a coefficient which is significant at the 5 percent level for a one-tail test. Neither he nor Graham report estimates for total fatalities. Nor do they report fatalities for motorcyclists despite Graham and Garber's earlier finding of a substantial adverse effect.

Thomas Zlatoper uses a regulation variable in his update of Peltzman's study for the 1947 to 1980 period.[30] As a proxy for regulated car safety features he uses a "pre-regulation" variable, the proportion of cars in operation of model years earlier than 1966. The pre-regulation variable is used in three regressions to explain total fatalities, vehicle occupant fatalities and pedestrian fatalities. For unknown reasons motorcyclist fatalities are grouped with vehicle occupants even though they are nonoccupants. Zlatoper's estimates imply that occupant fatalities are reduced by 13 percent and that total fatalities are reduced by 7 percent despite an 11 percent increase in pedestrian deaths.

Christopher Garbacz uses the same proxy as Zlatoper and reestimates the basic Peltzman equation.[31] The dependent variables are fatal accident rates per 100 million vehicle miles. For unknown reasons the period of analysis is 1952 to 1982 and omits the years 1947 to 1951. Garbacz's estimates imply that when 96 (38) percent of the cars have mandated safety equipment fatality rates are reduced by 73 (29) percent for occupants, 31 (12) percent for pedestrians and bicyclists, and 60 (23) percent overall. In 1982, 96 percent of cars had mandated equipment. He concludes that fatalities have been reduced with little or no offsetting behavior. We should be skeptical for two reasons. First, he too groups motorcyclists with occupants where adverse effects can be swamped by the safety effect for the larger group. Second, his estimates when all cars have mandated equipment are phenomenally high.

Robert Crandall, et al. (1986) extend the earlier analysis by Crandall and report several specifications of the fatality regressions including reanalysis of Peltzman's study.[32] The analysis in which they place the most confidence is the analysis of fatalities for 1947 to 1981. The key variable is the safety variable which measures the proportion of miles driven in cars built after 1965 weighted by Graham's estimates of crashworthiness. They find remarkably strong regulatory effects with total fatalities reduced by about 32 percent. However, they also find that nonoccupants are adversely affected and that the strength of the effect is nearly that of the regulation on all travelers taken together.

The key similarity in each of these seven recent studies is the use of a methodological approach which allows for human response to vehicle safety standards. They neither promote nor preclude by assumption any risk compensation. Essentially all seven are recent, refined studies which are consistent with our general, individual benefit-cost approach. They along with Peltzman's initial study consider the entire traffic system and estimate counterfactual fatality rates either by applying pre-regulation parameter estimates to the regulatory period or by using a regulatory variable over the entire period of study. The conclusions we can draw from these studies is the subject to which we now turn our attention.

INTERPRETING THE EVIDENCE

Safety Impacts of Vehicle Safety Standards – Conclusions

The studies which estimate the safety impacts of vehicle safety standards on fatality rates are summarized in Table 3-1. The table shows the estimated annual effects of regulation on the vehicle occupant fatality rate, nonoccupant (pedestrians, bicyclists and motorcyclists) fatality rate, and the total fatality rate. The annual lives saved is also reported for various years. Judgment has been used in selecting point estimates when only ranges were given by the author and in calculating lives saved when no total effect was given by the author.

Nonetheless, the table gives an accurate enough overview to exercise our judgment and draw four conclusions. Based on the evidence reviewed we can conclude:

- Occupants of passenger cars are safer. All studies find the vehicle occupant fatality rate is (or fatalities are) lower due to the vehicle safety regulation.
- Nonoccupants are in greater danger. All researchers except one find an indication of an increase in the fatality rate (or fatalities) for at least one group of nonoccupants

whether it be pedestrians, bicyclists or motorcyclists. Motorcyclists in particular are less safe because of the auto safety regulation.

- Overall highway and road travel is safer. The total fatality rate is lower due to the safety regulation. The overall increase in safety occurs despite the decrease in safety for nonoccupants. The safety-danger tradeoff among groups is such that the safety gain to the majority (occupants) outweighs the safety loss to the minority (nonoccupants).

- Occupants are probably less safe than technological studies promise. While the pattern in the evidence is less clear for this conclusion, it is supported by the decrease in safety for nonoccupants and the estimates of several studies.

We can illustrate the implications of these conclusions for the year 1984. If vehicle safety standards reduce car occupant fatalities by 15 percent, then the number of fatalities would have been 27,774 instead of 23,608. The number of car occupants saved is 4,166. If vehicle safety standards increase nonoccupant fatalities by 25 percent, then the number of fatalities would have been 9,841 instead of 12,301. The number of pedestrians, bicyclists and motorcyclists lost is 2,460. Overall, total traffic fatalities are 4 percent lower than they would have been without the regulation and net lives saved is 1,706.

Risk Compensation

Our conclusions that nonoccupants are in greater danger and occupants are not as much safer as technological studies promise mean that occupants have used some of the mandated safety increase for pursuit of other desirables. In other words we conclude that car safety regulation induced risk compensating behavior. The existence of risk compensation emphasizes the criticality of using a policy framework such as the individual cost-benefit approach. The approach considers the entire traffic safety system and allows for (without imposing) interactions among vehicle technology, highway/street conditions and the humans who use them. The idea of risk compensation is not new. Peltzman introduced the concept of offsetting behavior in his model of driver choice. Risk compensation is the essence of Wilde's risk homeostasis theory. Others have formulated similar concepts in their own research. Barry O'Neill allows for danger compensation in his decision theoretic model of accidents and Lloyd Orr discusses the same concept in his research on incentives and traffic safety.[33] Recently Leonard Evans framed risk compensation in what he

Table 3-1   IMPACT OF VEHICLE SAFETY STANDARDS ON TRAFFIC FATALITY RATES AND LIVES SAVED

Description of Study[a]	Estimated Annual Safety Change in Fatality Rate[b] Effects			Annual Lives Saved Net Total	Notes
	Occupants	Nonoccupants	Total		
1. Technological approach, Crash studies, Increases in crash survival probability, Various safety devices, Effect for 1972, Summary of numerous studies, Peltzman (1975:679–680)	-20%	0%	-16%	10,700	Accident chances are taken as. fixed. Lap seat belts and energy absorbing steering columns are the most important devices. There were 56,278 traffic fatalities in 1972. The estimate implies there would have been about 67,000 fatalities.
2. Individual net benefit approach, Econometric regression analysis, Fatal accident rates, National data for 1947–1972, Effect for 1972, Peltzman (1975:696)	-7%	(+36%)[c]	(+5%)	None	Primary factors are a long run safety trend, speed and a baby-boom youth effect.
3. Technological approach, Multiple regression analysis, Car model fatality rates per accident, North Carolina and New York data for 1966–1974 accidents, Effect for 1972, General Accounting Office (1976:34)	-25% (drivers) -12% (passengers)	0%	-8%	5,000	The study includes only cars involved in accidents.

Description of Study [a]	Estimated Annual Safety Effects Change in Fatality Rate [b]			Annual Lives Saved Net Total	Notes
	Occupants	Nonoccupants	Total		
4. Ad hoc empirical approach, Multiple regression analysis, Reanalysis of Peltzman's data, Effect for 1972, Robertson (1977:596)	-20%	-16%	-19%	12,900	Redefines variables. Makes theoretically arbitrary changes in regression equations. Finds a large decrease in nonoccupant fatalities. The estimate implies there would have been about 69,200 fatalities in 1972.
5. Individual net benefit approach, Econometric regression analysis, Update of Peltzman's study, National data for 1947–1977, Cantu (1980:55–56)	-13%	(+30%)	-0%	none	Refines and redefines some variables following his interpretation of Peltzman's theoretical model.
6. Technological approach, Multiple regression analysis, Car model fatal crash involvement rates, National data for 1975–1978, Effect for 1975–1978, average per year, Robertson (1981: 820)	-16%	-17%	-16%	9,300	Correlates found include vehicle age, vehicle age squared and vehicle age cubed. No driver characteristics are included.

Description of Study [a]	Estimated Annual Safety Effects Change in Fatality Rate [b]			Annual Lives Saved Net Total	Notes
	Occupants	Nonoccupants	Total		
7. Technological approach, multiple regression analysis, Reanalysis of Robertson's data, Effect for 1975–1978 Average per year, Orr (1984)	-%	(+%)	-2%	1,200	Deletes the truck rates and car-truck dummy variable because trucks are unregulated and the variable is highly correlated with regulation. An increase in motorcyclist fatalities appears to partly offset the decrease for car occupants.
8. Individual net benefit approach, Econometric regression analysis, Fatal accident rates, National data for 1947–1980, Effects for 1980, Graham and Garber (1984)	-23%	(+70%) (motorcyclists) 0% (pedestrians)	-14%	8,500	Regulation is measured by the proportion of miles driven in regulated cars. Motorcyclists are found to have a higher death rate because of care safety regulation. Bicyclists were not considered.
9. Individual net benefit approach, Econometric regression analysis, Fatalities for 1947–1980, Effect for 1980, Zlatoper (1984)	-13%	+11%	-7%	3,200	Regulation is measured by the proportion of cars in operation of model years earlier than 1966. Nonoccupants includes only pedestrians Motorcyclists are included with occupants.

Description of Study [a]	Estimated Annual Safety Effects Change in Fatality Rate [b]			Annual Lives Saved Net Total	Notes
	Occupants	Nonoccupant	Total		
10. Individual net benefit approach, Econometric regression analysis, Fatal accident rates, National data for 1947–1981, Effect for 1981, Crandall and Graham (1984)	-39%	(+%?)	-255	17,000	Regulation is measured by proportion of miles driven in cars built after 1967. Only pedestrians, not cyclists are considered. Lives saved includes only occupants.
11. Individual net benefit approach, Econometric regression analysis, fatalities for 1947–1981, Effect for 1981, Crandall and Graham (1984)	-54%	+18%	-38%	29,800	Regulation is measured by proportion of miles driven in cars built after 1965 weighted by estimates of improved occupant protection. Motorcyclists are not considered.
12. Individual net benefit approach, Econometric regression analysis, Fatal accident rates for 1952–1982, Effect for 1981, Garbacz (1985)	-73%	-31%	-60%	72,700	Regulation is measured by proportion of cars in operation of model years later than 1965. Motorcyclists are included with occupnats. Estimates imply total deaths in 1981 would have been 122,014.

| Description of Study [a] | Estimated Annual Safety Effects
Change in Fatality Rate [b] | | | Annual
Lives Saved
Net Total | Notes |
	Occupants	Nonoccupants	Total		
13. Individual net benefit approach, Eeconometric regression analysis, Fatal accidents for 1947–1981, Effect for 1981, Crandall *et al.* (1986)	-47%	(+61%) [c]	-32%	23,400	Regulation is measured by proportion of miles driven in cars built in 1965, weighted by estimates of improved occupant protection.

[a] Studies referred to are cited in the text.

[b] The studies typically report a range of estimated safety effects. At the risk of oversimplification only point estimates are given in this table. To characterize the various studies, judgement is used in selecting some point estimates and calculating total lives saved when no total estimate was given. Also in order to calculate safety effects for some studies, vehicle miles are assumed to be unaffected by safety devices. If vehicle miles are unaffected, then a percentage change in fatalities is the same as a percentage change in the fatality rate.

[c] Parentheses emphasize deleterious safety impacts.

calls "human behavior feedback."[34] The way in which an actual change in traffic systems relates to the intended or expected change depends on the human behavior feedback parameter. He reviews 26 studies of traffic safety studies including some of those included in Table 3-1 and reaches a conclusion similar to our own. He concludes that human behavior is pervasive in traffic systems and that behavior may greatly influence safety outcomes.

Risk compensation is possible within our individual benefit-cost framework and we conclude that risk compensation is an important factor which partly shapes the safety effects of auto safety regulation. Corroborative research lends confidence to this position.

Policy Evaluation and A Framework for Thinking

In Chapter 2, we compared the individual benefit-cost approach to the less general technological and risk homeostatic approaches and reviewed representative evidence on insurance, gambling, risk perception and safety belt use. We concluded the approach is useful for thinking about traffic safety policy. The evidence reviewed in this chapter led us to conclude that risk compensation exists in auto safety regulation and that policy benefits were overestimated. The evidence demonstrates that a general model such as ours must be used if formulation and evaluation of traffic safety policy is to be of high quality.

In this chapter we demonstrated the absurdity of NHTSA's claim that all of the 39 percent decline in the total fatality rate since 1966 can be attributed to its regulatory programs. We have seen instead that some of the decline can be attributed to NHTSA programs, but that other important factors exist as well. An optimistic current estimate is that some indication exists that NHTSA also is aware that a comprehensive framework is necessary for policy evaluation. In *Traffic Safety '84*, the successor to *Motor Vehicle Safety 1979*, NHTSA again describes the downward trend in the fatality rate since 1966 when federal traffic safety legislation was passed.[35] However, in the 1984 report only partial credit is claimed for the reduction in the fatality rate. Acknowledgment is given to many factors only one of which is the set of auto safety standards. An individual net benefit approach to traffic safety facilitates systematic consideration and analysis of all of the factors.

NOTES

[1] U. S. Department of Transportation. National Highway Traffic Safety Administration. *Motor Vehicle Safety 1979*. DOT HS 805 624. December 1980, p. iii.

[2] The fatality rates reported in Table 1-3 are for deaths attributable to a motor vehicle accident which occurs within one year of the accident. The decline using these rates is almost the same — 40 percent. If the rates based on deaths within 30 days of the accident are used, then the decline is 39 percent. See *Motor Vehicle Safety 1979* Table A-1, p. A-5.

[3] William Niskanen pointed out to me that the fatality rate as measured by traffic fatalities per 100 thousand population reflects a trend which is quite different from the vehicle mile rate. As shown in Table 3 in Chapter 1 the population traffic fatality rate fluctuates from year to year, but does not decline on average. It changes little from 22.8 in 1947 to 20.8 in 1961. The rate begins to increase in 1961, reaches a maximum of about 27 and stays at 27 until 1973. It then falls unsteadily to about 22 which is almost the same as the 1947 rate. (?)

[4] Sources reviewed include studies by the National Safety Council, NHTSA, U. S. Office of Science and Technology and numerous safety researchers. See Sam Peltzman. "The Effects of Automobile Safety Regulation." *Journal of Political Economy* 83 (August 1975): 677–725 especially pp. 678–680 and 718–721.

[5] See U. S. General Accounting Office. *Effectiveness, Benefits and Costs of Federal Safety Standards for Protection of Passenger Car Occupants*. Report to the U. S. Senate Committee on Commerce by the Comptroller General. CED 76 121. July 7, 1976.

[6] For a technical presentation of the approach and analysis see Sam Peltzman. "The Effects of Automobile Safety Regulation." (1975a). For a less technical, interpretive presentation see Sam Peltzman. *Regulation of Automobile Safety* (Washington, D.C.: American Enterprise Institute, 1975b).

[7] See Peltzman (1975a) pp. 680–693.

[8] See Peltzman (1975b) p. 12.

[9] See Peltzman (1975b) p. 17.

[10] See Peltzman (1975b) pp. 14–15.

[11] See Peltzman (1975b) pp. 3, 4, 18.

[12] See GAO (1976) p. 1.

[13] The conclusion is found in GAO (1976) pp. 12, 19 and 76.

[14] The reanalysis of Peltzman's data with some different variables is found in Leon S. Robertson "A Critical Analysis of Peltzman's The Effects of Automobile Safety Regulation." *Journal of Economic Issues* 11 (September 1977a): 587–600.

[15] See Leon S. Robertson "Rejoinder to Peltzman." *Journal of Economic Issues* 11 (September 1977b): 679–683 especially p. 681.

[16] See Robertson (1977a) p. 596.

[17] This comment is found in Sam Peltzman. "A Reply." *Journal of Economic Issues* 11 (September 1977): 672–679.

[18] The criticism is found in H. C. Joksch "Critique of Sam Peltzman's Study – The Effects of Automobile Safety Regulation" *Accident Analysis and Prevention* 8 (June 1976): 129–137. The quotation is from page 130.

[19] Economists have no monopoly on economic truth, but it is novel that noneconomist Joksch criticizes economist Peltzman for using the wrong measure of income.

[20] The point is that a data mass rarely "speaks for itself." A couple of general references are Carl Hempel. *Philosophy of Natural Science* (Englewood Cliffs, N.J.: Prentice-Hall, 1966) and Glenn E. Snelbecker. *Learning Theory, Instructional Theory and Psychological Design* (New York: McGraw Hill, 1974.)

[21] See Leon S. Robertson. "Automobile Safety Regulations and Death Reductions in the United States." *American Journal of Public Health* 71 (August 1981): 818–822.

[22] In earlier work Robertson analyzes fatal accident involvement rates where the rates are fatalities per registered vehicle for each model year of vehicle. The 1964–1967 models are found to have rates 20 percent lower than unregulated models and the post–1967 models have rates 39 percent less than the unregulated models. No significant effect on pedestrian fatalities is detected. See Leon S. Robertson "State and Federal New Car Safety Regulation: Effects on Fatality Rates" *Accident Analysis and Prevention* 9 (1977): 151–156.

[23] Robertson's findings are highly regarded within the public health community as evidenced by the curious endorsement of the editor of the *American Journal of Public Health* upon publication of the article: "Thus the study provides assurance that the specifics of the public health actions taken by the federal government were based on scientific knowledge and achieved their goal." Alfred Yankauer. "Deregulation and the Right to Life" *American Journal of Public Health* 71 (August 1981): 797–798.

[24] Lloyd D. Orr. "The Effectiveness of Automobile Safety Regulation: Evidence from the FARS Data" *American Journal of Public Health* 74 (1984): 1384–1389.

[25] Oscar R. Cantu. "An Updated Regression Analysis on the Effects of the Regulation of Auto Safety." Yale S.O.M. Working Paper No. 15 (May 1980).

[26] John D. Graham and Steven Garber. "Evaluating the Effects of Automobile Safety Regulation" *Journal of Policy Analysis and Management* 3 (Winter 1984): 206–224.

[27] The results of Graham's study are found in Robert W. Crandall and John D. Graham "Automobile Safety Regulation and Offsetting Behavior: Some New Empirical Estimates" *American Economic Review* 74 (May 1984): 328–331.

[28] According to demand theory the partial effect of an increase in the price of gasoline is to lower the quantity consumed. For one estimate of this relationship see Glenn Blomquist "The 55 MPH Speed Limit and Gasoline Consumption" *Resources and Energy* 6 (March 1984): 21–39.

[29] The results of Crandall's study are found in Crandall and Graham (1984).

[30] Thomas Zlatoper. "Regression Analysis of Time Series Data on the Motor Vehicle Deaths in the United States" *Journal of Transport Economics and Policy* 18 (September 1984): 263–274.

[31] Christopher Garbacz. "A Note on Peltzman's Theory of Offsetting Consumer Behavior" *Economic Letters* 19 (1985): 183–187.

[32] Robert W. Crandall, Howard K. Gruenspect, Theodore E. Keeler and Lester B. Lave. *Regulating the Automobile* (Washington, D.C.: The Brookings Institution, 1986).

[33] Barry O'Neill. "A Decision Theory Model and Danger Compensation" *Accident Analysis and Prevention* 9 (1977): 157–165 and Lloyd D. Orr. "Incentives and Efficiency in Automobile Safety Regulation" *Quarterly Review of Economics and Business* 22 (Autumn 1982): 43–65.

[34] Leonard Evans "Human Behavior Feedback and Traffic Safety" *Human Factors* 27 (October 1985): 555–576.

[35] U.S. Department of Transportation. National Highway Traffic Safety Administration. *Traffic Safety '84*. Preliminary Draft, p. 4.

CHAPTER 4

ECONOMICS OF MANDATORY PASSIVE RESTRAINTS: BENEFIT–COST ANALYSIS, RULEMAKING AND COURT DECISIONS

In contrast to overall, ex post evaluation of the entire set of vehicle safety standards, the subject of this chapter is ex ante evaluation of a single vehicle safety standard. Benefit cost analysis is a natural candidate for evaluating policy proposals. Mandatory passive restraints, the required installation of air bags or passive (automatic) safety belts, is a standard which has received a great deal of public and professional attention. The purpose of this chapter is twofold: to critically review recent benefit-cost analyses of mandatory passive restraints and to provide a general economic analysis of the passive restraints issue. The broader analysis encompasses two other parts of the regulatory process: administrative interpretation at the National Highway and Traffic Safety Administration and legal interpretation inherent in court decisions.

To keep the review and critique manageable the focus is on events during the 1980's. After background information is given, the studies and events of the 1980–1983 period including NHTSA's rescission of the passive restraints requirement and the overturning decision of the Supreme Court are analyzed in detail. Finally, the current standard which contains the Dole Rule for passive restraints and belt use laws is described and evaluated using five criteria recommended for judging analytical and economic acceptability of a safety standard.

BACKGROUND FOR CRASH PROTECTION RULES
AND COURT DECISIONS

The National Traffic and Motor Vehicle Safety Act of 1966 has at its core the promulgation of Federal Motor Vehicle Safety Standards which are designed to enhance automobile crashworthiness and reduce occupant injury due to the "second collision" between the occupant and the interior of the automobile. The original primary legal criteria give the guidelines for the standards: protect against unreasonable risks, state in terms of performance, be practicable in terms of technology and cost, provide objective compliance criteria.

The second criteria, which requires that a standard be stated in terms of performance rather than design, has played an important role in crash protection regulation. Because only performance can be required presumably NHTSA cannot require installation of specific equipment. A performance standard for occupant crash protection, for example, might state that occupants must be able to survive a 30 m.p.h. crash without serious injury and without extra effort. Manufacturers might comply by installing air bags, passive seat belts, or incorporating padded, energy-absorbing, user-friendly interiors. Manual seat belts would be unsatisfactory because they require effort in buckling. In exercising the considerable judgment required in development and promulgation of vehicle safety standards, NHTSA is bound by the Administrative Procedure Act of 1946 which requires public hearings. The hearings provide the opportunity for all interested parties to participate in the rulemaking process. Among the most controversial of the vehicle safety standards is Standard No. 208 "Occupant Crash Protection."

Federal Motor Vehicle Safety Standard Number 208 was one of the 20 initial vehicle safety standards issued in 1967. It required installation of lap and upper torso restraint belts in each front outboard seat of most cars and lap restraint belts in every other seating position. The requirement has changed several times over the last two decades. Manual seat belts were and are available in almost all cars in use but only a minority of passenger car occupants use belts. In order to increase usage for model year 1973 cars a continuous light and buzzer remained on until the front seat belts were fastened. Next, the seat belt-ignition interlock did induce an increase in safety belt use to 66 percent of 1974 model cars and 46 percent for 1975 models, but adverse public reaction to the mandated inconvenience and restriction which accompanied the belts and the fact that many people defeated the interlock system prompted Congress to void the interlock requirement. Since the ignition interlock reversal the requirement has been for a four to eight second light and buzzer combination which acts as a reminder to fasten safety belts.[1]

From the outset attempts were made to introduce new technology for occupant protection in the form of passive restraints. In July 1969 an advanced notice of Proposed Rulemaking entitled "Inflatable Occupant Restraint Systems" introduced the idea of "air bags" which would inflate during an accident to cushion occupants during the "second collision" between the occupant and the inside part of the car. The attractive feature of this safety device is that an individual can be passive since no action such as buckling is required of the occupants. A passive restraint standard was issued in 1971 but was overturned by the court until a suitable dummy could be developed for testing the performance of the restraints.

During the next few years while there was uncertainty concerning the safety standard, some autos were manufactured with passive restraints. General Motors sold about 10,000 Buicks, Oldsmobiles and Cadillacs with airbags. Volkswagen sold about 75,000 Rabbits with passive belts. Mercury and Volvo sold a few cars equipped with airbags. Most cars came equipped with manual (active) safety belt systems, not passive restraints. In December 1976 after again considering a mandatory passive restraint standard, former Secretary of Transportation William T. Coleman attempted to defuse the controversy with a compromise. Proponents cited the great potential for reducing death and injury, while opponents raised questions about effectiveness, reliability, cost, loss of individual freedom and public acceptance.

The Coleman Rule called for a continuation of mandated safety belt installation but created a demonstration program to familiarize the public with passive restraints. Contracts were negotiated with four manufacturers for 500,000 cars equipped with passive restraints for model years 1980 and 1981. The rationale for the program was that passive restraints were technologically feasible, could be effective in reducing traffic deaths and injuries and could be produced at a reasonable cost. The rationale for not mandating passive restraints was threefold:

- Adverse public reaction might lead to another congressional reversal as in the cases of ignition interlocks and mandatory motorcycle helmet use, and an apparently promising technological advance would be lost.

- Passive restraints are more costly than other safety
  equipment, and the public deserves a better documented
  case for costly standards than with inexpensive standards
  especially when some occupants would be giving up active
  safety belts which are known to work well.
- There may be increases in the voluntary consumer
  demand for passive restraints due to the demonstration
  program. There was also the possibility that use of active
  safety belts might increase making passive restraints
  redundant.

With the change in administration incoming Secretary of Transportation
Brock Adams abandoned the Coleman Rule on the bases that public
acceptance is not part of the traffic safety mandate, passive restraints clearly
will be effective in improving traffic safety and the cost of the restraints will be
more than offset through savings on insurance premium payments. In June
1977 under the Adams Rule, passive restraints were mandated for standard
and luxury cars by the 1982 model year, for intermediate and compact size cars
by the 1983 model year, and for subcompact and mini-size cars by the 1984
model year. The Adams Rule survived congressional and judicial review.[2]

In April of 1981, under a new administration and new Secretary of
Transportation Drew Lewis, Vehicle Safety Standard No. 208 was amended to
delay until model year 1983 the requirement for passive restraints in large cars.
The primary argument for the delay was that since most manufacturers were
planning to use passive belts, not airbags, and were shifting away from large
cars, the occupant restraint standard should be reassessed. In October 1981
NHTSA rescinded the mandatory passive restraints rule. During the
rulemaking process benefit-cost analysis was used to support different
positions on the merits of the proposed rescission. We turn to examine the
nature of these studies and their results.

BENEFIT-COST STUDIES OF MANDATORY PASSIVE RESTRAINTS

Economics offers a framework for balancing the advantages and
disadvantages of vehicle safety standards so as to promote the greatest good
for the greatest number. Through benefit-cost analysis it is possible to identify
the tradeoffs inherent in a vehicle safety standard. At its best it facilitates
estimation of the amount of other traffic safety programs, public health
programs, cancer research, national defense, and private consumption which

must be forgone to obtain an increase in occupant safety. In principle benefit-cost analysis can identify vehicle safety standards which can produce gains which are large enough that the losses to the net losers could be fully covered by the gains to the net beneficiaries with gains left over. The benefit-cost framework is relevant to NHTSA's decisions, because conceptually it offers a method for balancing the advantages and disadvantages of vehicle safety standards; for determining when the accident risk is acceptable and reasonable and when the standard is practicable in cost.

An Ideal Study

A sketch of an exemplary study illustrates what should be contained in a benefit-cost analysis of mandatory passive restraints if it is to be useful:

- The estimates should reflect changes over what would have existed without the standard. Increases and decreases from the current state are relevant.

- Benefits should reflect any reduction in fatalities and injuries and the values of the reductions. Any reductions should reflect changes in chances of survival in accidents compared to existing usage of manual safety belts and any changes in the chances of an accident. The value of any reductions in risks should reflect people's willingness to pay.

- Costs should reflect any costs of installation of equipment which would not have been installed and any increases in operation costs borne by vehicle users.

Conventional benefit-cost analysis has been used to attempt to help determine the overall social desirability of mandatory passive restraints. The Adams Rule (mandatory airbags or detachable passive belts) was accompanied by an analysis in which NHTSA concluded that positive net benefits would be associated with the standard. NHTSA estimated that 9,000 traffic fatalities and 65,000 injuries would be prevented each year. Two years later the General Accounting Office reviewed the NHTSA analysis, agreed that passive restraints offered potential for increasing traffic safety, but challenged NHTSA's point estimates and emphasized that the range implied negative net benefits were possible also.[3] With these older studies providing a background four new benefit-cost studies were prepared as the Adams Rule was questioned and rescission was considered. Two of the studies were made specifically for the rulemaking decision and two were made independently just prior to the hearings.

Arnould and Grabowski

The first independent attempt to estimate conventionally the benefits and costs of mandatory passive restraints was made by Richard Arnould and Henry Grabowski.[4] For the reduction in fatalities and injuries in crashes they use two sets of estimates. One set is based on a 1981 field team study of rural traffic accidents which shows, for example that fatalities are reduced by 34 percent by air bags and lap belts together, 32 percent by lap and shoulder belts together, 28 percent by passive belts, and 25 percent by air bags alone.[5] The field study estimates are only approximately one half of the NHTSA lab study estimates which is the other set. Arnould and Grabowski assume that 60 to 70 percent of occupants with passive belts would use them and that 0 to 20 percent of occupants with air bags would also use lap belts. Occupant protection is assumed to have no affect on chances of accidents. The 1975 distribution of traffic accident injuries and the estimates of restraint effectiveness in crashes are used to calculate the fatalities and injuries prevented.

Values of the estimated reductions in risk of death and injury were based on amounts which individuals implicitly reveal they are willing to pay for risk reduction. Citing a study by Martin Bailey they use a value of $300 for a risk reduction of .001, or as it is sometimes expressed a value of lifesaving of $300,000, (1975 values).[6] Adjustment for medical and legal cost externalities are made. A weighting scheme which expresses values of injuries ranging from critical to minor as a fraction of the value for a fatality. The estimates of the costs of passive belts and air bags are based on industry estimates and are approximately $50 and $225 respectively.

In steady-state equilibrium the annual total social costs of passive belts are estimated to be from $0.5 to 1.0 billion dollars per year and the same type of costs of air bags are estimated to be from $2.5 to 6.5 billion dollars per year depending on which cost estimates are used. Comparable benefits are estimated to be from $2.1 to 5.5 billion dollars per year for passive belts and $3.6 to 6.4 billion dollars per year for air bags. Costs and benefits are expressed in 1975 dollars. For passive belts the estimated net benefits are positive for each case examined. For air bags, the net benefits are smaller and always negative for the better costs estimates. Arnould and Grabowski conclude that passive belts are a much more cost effective approach to occupant crash protection than air bags.

Graham, Henrion and Morgan

John Graham, Max Henrion and Granger Morgan estimate the net benefits of mandatory passive restraints as part of an analysis of several policy options concerning occupant restraints.[7] Their analysis builds on existing estimates and in ways is quite similar to Arnould and Grabowski. Two distinguishing features of the analysis are the explicit use of expert, subjective probablistic judgment in estimating key parameters and the precise reporting of the effects of uncertainty in sensitivity analysis.

They use existing estimates of restraint effectiveness in crashes and a fixed distribution of traffic accidents as do Arnould and Grabowski. For safety belt use, however, they use a different technique. They asked a panel of 5 specialists in occupant-crash protection what they thought the percentage of occupants belted in crashes for fleets of cars with detachable passive belts would be. The composite median usage was 17 percent with a composite "lower bound" (.1 fractile) of 10 percent and a composite "upper level" (.9 fractile) of 35 percent. The panel of specialists was asked the same question for "discourage-defeat" passive belts which are not easily detached. The composite median usage for the more coercive belt system was 43 percent with a lower bound of 15 percent and an upper bound of 60 percent.

Based on the median belt usage of 17 percent for passive belts Graham et al. estimated that the net benefits of mandatory passive belts, the Adams Rule, are approximately $1.0 billion per year (1981 dollars). The explanation for the positive net benefits even with the relatively low usage is that the value of risk reduction, the value of lifesaving of $700,000 is approximately double the value used by Arnould and Grabowski. The estimates of net benefits turn out to be as sensitive to the value of lifesaving as to safety belt usage. Several alternatives to the Adams Rule are also evaluated and found to have positive net benefits. Two of the other policy options and the estimated annual net benefits in billions of 1981 dollars are: air bags alone (5.1) and "nondetachable" passive belts (3.4). Graham, Henrion and Morgan also conclude that at least one form of mandatory passive restraints will yield positive net social benefits.

Final Regulatory Impact Analysis by NHTSA

In October 1981 NHTSA published the final regulatory impact analysis upon which the rescission of mandatory passive (automatic) occupant restraints was based.[8] The basic approach in analysis of the safety benefits and dollar costs is similar to that of earlier studies and some of the same data is used to make estimates. The text of the 1981 NHTSA document and the benefit-cost analysis found in Appendix A of the report permit comparison of these studies. A notable difference is that the 1981 analysis focuses on passive belts and hardly considers air bags. (This sleight of air bags is crucial in the subsequent Supreme Court decision.) The reason given is the great shift from large to small cars in the vehicle fleet. NHTSA estimates that small (compact and subcompact) cars will account for 67 percent of new car sales for model year 1985 up from 44 percent in 1978. Due to design and cost advantages in small cars manufacturers plan to install passive belts rather than air bags.

Effectiveness of belts in preventing injury is based on analysis of data from the National Crash Severity Study and crash tests. Passive belts are assumed to be equivalent to the effectiveness of the manual 3–point belt. To estimate the safety benefits of passive belts NHTSA relies heavily on data from the Fatal Accident Reporting System and the National Accident Sampling System. Projections are made for the mix of the stock of autos and are combined with fatality and injury data for 1980 and 1979. The accident probability distribution (chances of accidents) is assumed to be unaffected by the occupant restraint rule. Since the passive belts would be detachable to permit emergency egress and mitigate adverse consumer response the key parameter is safety belt usage. Arnould and Grabowski assumed that belt usage would be 60 to 70 percent based primarily on the experience with Volkswagen Rabbits.

NHTSA estimates that 60 percent belt usage is the maximum that one could hope for with passive belts and that the minimum is 23 percent, approximately double the 1981 average usage. NHTSA judged that the 60 to 70 percent usage was too high because: current systems had ignition interlocks or were nondetachable, VW owners have an atypically high demand for safety belts and usage in subcompacts is not a good predictor of usage in larger cars. Based on the difference in belt usage between cars equipped with manual and those equipped with passive belts the mean of total usage is estimated to be 52 percent. Based on the ratio multiplier of the belt usage in cars with passive belts to cars with manual belts the mean of total belt usage is estimated to be 29 percent. This usage is still greater than median value of 17 percent used by Graham et al. though it is within their range of 10 to 35 percent.

Annual traffic fatalities prevented range in steady state from 2,050 if belt use is 23 percent to 8,750 if belt use is 60 percent. The higher estimate is quite close to that of Arnould and Grabowski for NHTSA's estimate of effectiveness. The valuation of the safety benefits is based on a foregone earnings approach instead of the willingness to pay, and the values of risk reduction are lower than in other studies.[9]

The cost estimates for passive belts are based primarily on manufacturers' figures which range from $50 to $150 dollars. NHTSA estimates that the average long run, steady state incremental cost of passive belts is $75 per car. There is also an extra fuel cost of $14 per car per year due to 10 additional pounds of weight. The point estimate of total steady state cost is $1.0 billion with a range from 0.7 to 1.3 billion dollars in 1981 dollars.

NHTSA estimates the annual long run, steady state net benefits of passive belts are probably between $0.9 to 3.7 billion in 1981 dollars. The results of the benefit-cost analysis are reported in terms of break – even usage of passive belts and a graph showing net social benefits. The break-even usage rates range from 20 percent to 30 percent depending on the method and discount rate used for valuing risk reductions. The net benefits are positive but small if the 29 percent belt usage is representative. NHTSA emphasized the 30 percent break even usage rate and the small difference at the projected 29 percent usage. It was noted that actual usage of passive belts could be as low as 23 percent and that usage of manual belts might increase enough to make passive belts superfluous.

Nordhaus' Revision of NHTSA's Analysis

In his testimony on the rescission of the Adams Rule William Nordhaus gave a critique of NHTSA's benefit-cost analysis and offered an alternative study.[10] His critique covers numerous topics including the estimated cost of passive belts and the value of risk reductions employed. The central issue, however is the projected increase in usage which would accompany passive safety belts.

Nordhaus observes that the conventional (NHTSA) approach is to assume that the increase in belt usage will be additive. With the additive model the difference between cars with passive belts and with manual belts is added to current usage for all occupant and vehicle groups. Adding the average incremental usage of 41 percentage points to the current average usage of 11 percent yields a total average usage of 52 percent. Nordhaus argues that the additive (difference) approach is statistically superior to the ratio (multiplicative) approach favored by NHTSA. The ratio approach assumes that the proportion by which usage increases for each occupant group is the same. The ratio approach implies that the current rates will approximately double; the average total usage according to the multiplicative approach is 29 percent. Calculations aside, Nordhaus' gist is that the point estimate of average usage of passive belts of 52 percent is at least as good as the lower estimate. Furthermore, the social net benefits of mandatory passive restraints are positive with 52 percent of occupants using the passive belts. Based on the NHTSA analysis of benefits and costs the social net benefits at 52 percent belt usage range from approximately 1.1 to 3.5 billion dollars per year. Nordhaus estimates that the long run, steady state net benefits of mandatory passive restraints are approximately $2.4 billion per year.

Nordhaus also analyzes the benefits of alternatives to the Adams Rule which calls for large car first phase-in of passive restraints. These alternatives are simultaneous installation of passive restraints in cars of all sizes, reversal of the phase in so that small cars have passive restraints first, and rescission. Of these the small-car-first alternative has slightly larger net benefits than the Adams Rule, or simultaneous installation and much larger net benefits than rescission.

The major features of the four benefit-cost analyses discussed are summarized in Table 4-1. While differences exist, they share a common result. We might offer a conclusion based on these conventional benefit cost studies that the mandatory passive restraints policy as described in the Adams Rule passes the social net benefit test.

To draw such a conclusion, however, would be unwarranted. Confidence in the result mandatory passive restraints are socially desirable must be tempered by recognition that crucial factors have been ignored in these four studies. The problem is not the treatment of safety belt usage which was done thoughtfully. Rather, the problem is the assumptions made, implicitly or explicitly, which are inconsistent with the general individual benefit-cost framework. This approach was helpful in thinking about the design of appropriate traffic safety policy and evaluation of the contribution of vehicle safety to reductions in traffic fatality rates. The approach is now useful in assessing these conventional benefit-cost analyses.

CRITIQUE OF THE BENEFIT-COST ANALYSIS

Recall that an exemplary benefit-cost analysis of mandatory passive restraints should reflect changes in the chances of survival in accidents and any changes in the chances of accidents. The analysis should reflect costs of installation of equipment and any increases in operation costs borne by vehicle users. The general problem with the studies reviewed is that they have taken a technological approach to traffic safety. An individual net benefit approach, which is consistent with the exemplary social benefit-cost analysis, suggests two critical areas of inadequacy. The studies fail to incorporate estimates of changes in chances of accidents due to motorist response and user costs of passive safety belts associated with discomfort and inconvenience.

Table 4-1   BENEFIT-COST STUDIES OF MANDATORY PASSIVE RESTRAINTS

Description	Air Bags	Passive Safety Belts	Manual Safety Belts	Benefit Values	Costs	Annual Net Benefits
Air bags and passive belts, 1975 dollars, Arnould and Grabowski (1981)	Reduce fatalities by 25%–50%	Reduce fatalities by 28%–56%, Use should be 60%–70%	Lap and shoulder belts reduce fatalities by 32%–64%, Use of lap belts with air bags would be 0–20%	$300,000 per statistical life	Air bags: $225 Passive Belts: $50	Air bags: $-2.0 to +3.9 billion Passive belts: $1.1–5.0 billion
Air bags and passive belts, 1981 dollars, Graham, Henrion and Morgan (1981)		Use would be 10%–35%, 17% average		$700,000 per statistical life		Air bags: $5.1 billion Passive belts: $1.0 billion

Description	Air Bags	Passive Safety Belts	Manual Safety Belts	Benefit Values	Costs	Annual Net Benefits
Passive belts, 1981 dollars, NHTSA (1981)	Since most new car sales will involve cars with passive belts, air bags are not analyzed.	Use would be 23% to 60%, 29% used (less than 100% because of detachment)	Increase in future use reduces net benefits of passive belts to 0	$310,000 per statistical life	Passive belts: $50 –$150	Passive belts: $0.9–$3.7 billion
Passive belts, 1981 dollars, Nordhaus (1981)	Same as NHTSA (1981)	Use would be 52%		$480,000 per statistical life	Passive belts: $114 used	Passive belts: $1.1–3.5 billion

Accidents Chances are Assumed Constant — No Human Response

Although attention has been given to belt usage following the requirement for passive restraints other human response has been ignored. Each of the studies assumes that the distribution and severity of crashes is unaffected. This means that all travelers will continue to travel under the same conditions in the same manner as before, after automobiles are equipped with passive restraints. In other words, the assumption is that drivers and other travelers are passive towards passive restraints and do not change their travel choices, driving or safety-related behavior. The assumption applies not only to those drivers of cars already equipped with passive belts such as some Volkswagen Rabbits and Chevettes or cars with airbags, but also drivers who have chosen not to purchase these cars which are equipped with passive restraints.

The assumption of traveler passivity biases conventional benefit-cost studies towards positive net benefits. The reason for the bias in favor of safety equipment is that reasonable substitutions (risk compensation) can lead to more accidents and more violent accidents. The consequences are that the decrease in occupant fatalities will be less than expected based on technological effectiveness and that there will be an increase in nonoccupant injuries.

The upward bias is inherent in a technological approach to traffic safety. The rigid approach caused problems in measuring the contribution of vehicle safety regulation export and it causes problems for evaluating mandatory passive restraints ex ante. The individual net benefit approach is a better approach because it incorporates zero risk compensation as a special case and permits attempts to measure any risk compensation.

Although human response may be the most difficult parameter to estimate it is potentially the most important. Consider the pivotal role that safety belt usage played in the four analysis. Results turned on usage — a human factor. In general the studies succeeded in incorporating this dimension of individual behavior into the benefit-cost analysis. Similar effort must be made to incorporate changes in the traffic environment by establishing a range of change in the chances of accidents — not only for occupants, but for nonoccupants as well.

Substitutability Among Policy Components

A complicating interaction not considered analysis is how passive restraints affect other components of traffic safety policy. Conventional procedures treat policy components as having isolated, independent impacts on effectiveness in crashes. But with multi-component policy packages of interrelated impacts the values of package components are not necessarily unique. The value of the component depends on its order or place in the policy package. In the case where there is a large number of policy impacts, such as with motor vehicle safety standards and highway safety programs, the error in valuing each component separately is probably systematic. Because of substitutability among components, the net benefits of any part valued independently and first are overstated. For example, passive restraints reduce the value of nonlacerating windshields, the 55 m.p.h. speed limit, and according to one study, crash attenuators in front of bridge piers.[11] The additional safety to be gained from passive restraints are probably overestimated if they are estimated in isolation. The failure to consider substitutability among policy components and the failure to include increases in accident chances for all travelers due to risk compensation both bias the estimate of benefits upward. The benefits are exaggerated.[12]

Implicit User Costs — Another Human Factor

An exemplary benefit-cost analysis would include any changes in operation costs borne by vehicle users. A limitation of all four of the benefit cost studies reviewed is that they ignore changes in implicit user costs. By ignoring additional user costs, costs are underestimated and the estimate of net benefit of mandatory passive restraints is biased upward. Implicit user costs are real costs even though they do not involve money expenditure. In benefit-cost analyses of other traffic-related programs implicit user costs have been estimated for years. For example, a reduction in travel time costs has been acknowledged as a major benefit of road investments. Conceptually it makes no difference whether there is a change in implicit user costs associated with expressway travel-time savings and greater convenience — or a change associated with safety belts — less comfort, less convenience, time lost. The costs are real social costs and should be included.

Implicit costs are recognized by motorists. Recall that motorists cite discomfort and inconvenience as a major deterrent to safety belt use. My own research indicates that discomfort costs are more than 7 times as large as time costs for manual lap belts.[13] Individuals are considering implicit user costs in their own private assessment.

The mistake of omitting implicit user costs is not new nor is it peculiar to the passive restraint issue. The Highway Safety Needs Report ranks various highway safety countermeasures by cost-effectiveness and finds:

Two countermeasures, mandatory seat belt usage the the national 55 mph speed limit, stand out above all others as having very large payoffs at relatively small unit investments. Moreover, the data on which the cost effectiveness of these two measures is based on equal to or superior to that which supports any other proposed measure.[14]

Schizophrenically, the report notes that there is public resistance perhaps because not all costs have been considered. If the DOT estimate of $1 billion per year in time costs (found in the appendix of the report) is taken into account the speed limit drops from the fourth best to the 22nd best countermeasure. If time costs are considered, compulsory safety belt usage drops from best to fifth best, and if disutility costs are considered the law drops to the 25th best countermeasure.[15] Undoubtedly mandatory motorcycle helmet usage would drop a great deal from its rank of 13th if rider disutility costs were included. These traffic safety programs are highly recommended even though DOT acknowledges that implicit user costs are ignored.[16] Others too perceive that this practice is common in cost-effectiveness studies of traffic safety improvements even though it goes against a long tradition of including user time costs in analysis of highway projects.[17] To show that any component of traffic safety policy, including mandatory passive restraints, is socially cost-effective, all costs must be included whether or not they are pecuniary.

Indirectly, implicit user costs do bear on the decisions at NHTSA, but with quite different results. If public resistance to the restraint standard increases with implicit user costs then each of the last three major decisions by NHTSA reflect cognizance of implicit costs. Secretary of Transportation Coleman devised a demonstration program to test and enhance consumer acceptance, Secretary Adams dismissed the Coleman Rule and required passive restraints on the basis that public acceptance does not matter, and Secretary Lewis rescinded the requirement citing potential adverse consumer reaction. Viewed in this light all three secretaries had to deal with implicit costs. Ultimately administrative judgment will be required on passive restraints but explicit incorporation of user costs into benefit-cost analysis is conceptually appropriate. In one sense it is as a measure of public resistance.

The decision to rescind the Adams Rule was not made counter to results of an exemplary benefit-cost analysis which show positive net benefits of mandatory passive restraints. Taken together the four studies reviewed show positive net benefits, but they are not exemplary because they ignored crucial factors. The studies are biased in favor of a passive restraints rule because: accident chances will be greater for occupants and nonoccupants – not fixed, other safety devices will not be as effective because of substitutability, and implicit user costs will be greater due to discomfort and inconvenience with passive belts. The conclusions of the last chapter that the fatality reductions from standards is smaller than expected and the public resistance to safety belts indicate that these are nontrivial factors.[18] They illustrate the mistakes which can be avoided by thinking about traffic safety using an individual net benefit approach. The approach guides exemplary benefit-cost analysis and formulation of appropriate policy proposals. Further the approach provides a helpful perspective on the myriad of regulatory and legal decisions surrounding occupant restraint rulemaking.

PERSPECTIVE ON REGULATORY AND LEGAL DECISIONS

Rescission and the Courts

Given NHTSA's emphasis on the case of little net benefit in its analysis it is not surprising that the mandatory passive restraints rule was rescinded in October 1981. The reasons given were:

- automobile manufacturer's plans had changed since 1977 so that compliance would result in passive belts being installed instead of airbags;
- the prediction that there would be little increase in safety belt use because the passive belts could be detached easily; and
- the potential for adverse consumer reaction which might adversely affect the entire safety program.[19]

In 1982, when asked to review the NHTSA decision to withdraw the requirement for installation of passive restraints, the United States Court of Appeals for the District of Columbia Circuit gave the rescission a hostile reception. The court of appeals found the rescission to be arbitrary and capricious for three reasons:

- there was insufficient evidence that there would be no increase in protection through increased seat belt usage;
- inadequate consideration was given to nondetachable passive belts; and
- complete failure to give any consideration to an airbags-only standard.

In addition to finding this procedural inadequacy the court of appeals interpreted legislative activity over the previous nine years to constitute a congressional commitment to passive restraints and concluded that the rescission by NHTSA raised doubts about the agency's effort to fulfill its mandate.[20]

The Supreme Court agreed to hear arguments on the case of the *Motor Vehicle Manufacturers Association of the United States, Inc. v. State Farm Mutual Automobile Insurance Company* and on June 24, 1983 rendered its decision. The Supreme Court identified the ultimate question as whether NHTSA's rescission of the passive restraint requirement was arbitrary and capricious. It concluded, as did the court of appeals, that in terms of procedural adequacy the rescission was arbitrary and capricious because NHTSA failed to supply the requisite, reasoned analysis, but it did not accept all of the reasoning of the court of appeals.

The Supreme Court cited two notable deficiencies in NHTSA's justification for rescission. Both deficiencies are omissions from NHTSA's analysis. The first deficiency is the absence of consideration given to an alternative which would require airbags. The Court noted that there was not one sentence in NHTSA's rulemaking statement which discusses the airbag-only option. The second deficiency is that NHTSA failed to articulate an argument against developing a standard which would require non-detachable passive safety belts. The Court was concerned that the agency grouped continuous (spool) passive seat belts together with ignition interlocks and failed to offer any explanation why the continuous belt would induce the same negative public response as interlocks. On nonconformity to administrative procedure, the pivotal legal issue, the Court agreed with the Court of Appeals.[21]

The Court of Appeals, based on its own assessment of legislative occurrences, inferred a congressional commitment to the concept of automatic crash protection devices for vehicle occupants. Its assessment raised doubts about NHTSA's effort to fulfill its statutory mandate. The court of appeals stated that as a consequence the agency was obligated to supply increasingly clear and convincing reasoning. The Supreme Court found, however, that this path of analysis was misguided and questionable. The Court pointed out that other contemporaneous events could be read as illustrating equal congressional opposition to passive restraints. Regardless of which reading is more accurate the Supreme Court determined that the inferences to be drawn from legislative occurrences fail to suggest that NHTSA's rescission of mandatory passive restraints was improper with respect to the standard of review, procedural adequacy.

The opinion of the Supreme Court was not unanimous. Justice Rehnquist, joined by Justice Burger and Justices Powell and O'Connor, concurred in part and dissented in part. The minority agreed that NHTSA should have given explanations for not leaving intact the requirement for airbags or continuous spool passive belts. They did not agree that the decision concerning the detachable passive belts was arbitrary and capricious. They found it reasonable for NHTSA to decide that studies do not support any conclusion about use of seat belts that are installed in cars whether the consumer wants them or not and whether belts are linked to an ignition interlock or not. These justices also emphasized a point made in the majority's opinion that a court is not to substitute its judgment for that of the agency and that the agency's judgment may change over time. They observed that NHTSA's view of Vehicle Safety Standard 208 changed with Presidential administrations and that members of one administration may consider public resistance and uncertainties more important than members of other administrations. They offered the insight that changes in agency judgment brought about by changes in administrations brought about by people casting their votes is perfectly reasonable. Furthermore this democratic change is a reasonable basis for an executive agency's reappraisal of the benefits and costs of its regulations.[22]

In other words the minority opinion reveals judicial skepticism concerning the degree with which delegation of power and administrative government removes politics from regulatory decisions. The position seems to indicate that the decision is inevitably partly political and that it is unreasonable to expect NHTSA to limit its consideration to only certain types of scientific evidence. It is more reasonable to expect the agency to weigh many factors as long as it remains within the bounds of the law.

Legal Decisions, Regulatory Decisions and Economic Analysis

After reviewing the bases for the decisions of the court of appeals, the Supreme Court and the rationale for the minority opinion, clearly there is agreement that the determining factor in the case of passive restraints was procedural adequacy with respect to administrative law. By failing to give any consideration to an airbag-only requirement or a nondetachable passive belts requirement, NHTSA failed to comply with the mandated administrative procedure. In this sense the decision of the agency was arbitrary and capricious.

The label, however, does not apply to economic analysis in regulatory decisions about traffic safety. In fact the Court said that NHTSA was correct to look at the costs as well as the benefits of the passive restraints standard. The

Court even offers its own view on the net benefits of seat belt use. Despite the stated acceptance, the Court's approach to costs and benefits of traffic safety measures is puzzling from an economic perspective. While accepting the idea that costs of passive restraints are relevant to NHTSA's decision, the Court reminds the agency that safety shall be the overriding consideration. While saying that the net benefits of seat belt use are undoubtedly positive, the Court restricts consideration to monetary costs. Thus even though the 1983 decision of the Court turned on procedural adequacy and not on analytical adequacy, analytical adequacy and benefit-cost analysis were discussed.[23]

In the future, economic analysis can be useful to NHTSA in building a reasonable explanation for its decision on passive restraints and can be useful to the Court in the determining of adequacy when there is at least nominal compliance with administrative law. The potential contribution of an individual benefit-cost approach and economic analysis to this traffic safety issue is worth considering.

Any review of NHTSA decisions about vehicle safety standards must recognize the assumption on which the safety mandate is based and the judgment required to interpret the directions given. The fundamental assumption is that there are too many traffic injuries and that regulatory action must be taken to reduce them to an acceptable level. The stated purpose of the Vehicle Safety Act is to reduce traffic accidents and death and injury from traffic accidents; the assumption is that losses without the law are unacceptable. Motor vehicle safety is defined in the statute as vehicle performance which protects persons against unreasonable risks; the assumption is that vehicle safety standards will reduce the risks to a reasonable level. Standards are supposed to be practicable in terms of several factors including the ultimate cost (if any) to the consumer.

In view of the Herculean task of determining what number of injuries is not "too many," what level of injuries is acceptable, and what level of risk is reasonable, some leeway must be given to NHTSA in making decisions about safety standards. In its decision the Supreme Court recognizes the difficulty NHTSA faces. At the outset the Court indicated that while current loss of life on our highways is unacceptably high, improving safety does not admit to easy solution. An individual benefit-cost approach offers an explanation as to why there is no easy solution and why there is controversy surrounding the mandatory passive restraint rule.

The political interpretation of the traffic safety goals and vehicle safety regulations is clear — enough people thought they would gain, so they formed coalitions to secure safety legislation; the economic interpretation of the goals and regulations is less clear. Indeed the statute itself appears to deny the basic law of scarcity. Two signs point to denial of scarcity. One sign is that in contrast to frequent declarations that the cost of accidents is too high, there is no discussion of the ideal level of accident costs and why nonregulatory reality departs from that ideal. The other sign is that the cost appears to be an afterthought in the original primary criteria for the standards. The denial of scarcity poses a problem for regulators because when standards are promulgated someone inevitably incurs a cost and that party may object.

The loss of vehicle occupant lives on the highways could probably be reduced below the level possible with passive restraints alone if motor vehicles were equipped with airbags and also passenger belt harnesses similar to those worn by aircraft pilots, rollbar cages similar to those found in race cars, heavy-duty metal vehicle bodies, radar—controlled brakes, and a governor which limits speed to 35 m.p.h. These safety measures might effectively reduce the loss of lives of vehicle occupants, but few people would consider the accompanying costs to be reasonable. The costs in lifestyle through changes in commuting, vacations, family reunions and the costs in lost production through changes in sales, distribution and firm location would be substantial in addition to the increases in purchase price and operating costs of the vehicle.

One reason for the resistance to airbags is that the estimated cost to the consumer is an order of magnitude greater than the cost of other safety standards. Current crashworthiness standards, of course, are not as extreme as the hypothetical example, but little in the mandate or primary legal criteria indicates the example is extreme. Apparently, only agency administrative judgment and general political considerations prevent the hypothetical extreme.[24]

Judging Analytical Acceptability — Five Criteria

Since considerable judgment must be exercised by NHTSA to make a good decision on passive restraints and further judgment must be exercised by the courts in determining the adequacy of the reasoning supplied by the agency for the decision, it is useful to examine the implications of an economic approach to traffic safety. NHTSA should answer several questions if it is to provide a sound basis for its decision. The courts and the public might well consider it essential that these questions be addressed if the analysis and explanation for the regulatory decision are to be found acceptable.

1. **Are Overall Benefits and Costs Considered?** Exemplary benefit-cost analysis, which incorporates human factors, can be helpful in measuring the overall tradeoff between safety which may accompany passive restraints and

other worthy goals which must be sacrificed. Whether formal benefit-cost analysis is used or not there should be some recognition of scarcity in the regulatory rationale and some method for determining when accident risk is acceptable. The alternative to this balanced, practical approach is enslavement to a safety imperative which knows no bounds and creates innumerable conflicts.

2. Are Imperfections in Motorists' Decisions Weighed Against Regulatory Imperfections? The regulatory analysis should identify the causes of the deficiencies in motorists individual benefit-cost analyses, determine the extent of any shortcomings and determine the size of any consequent social problem. This investigation into imperfections is important because it provides a check on any formal, social benefit-cost analysis (exemplary or not) and it provides clues as to which policy tool is best suited to the problem. Because it is costly to promulgate vehicle safety standards and because the specific form of regulation may needlessly restrict some consumers' choices and change some producers' revenues the imperfect situation with the regulation should be compared to reliance upon drivers' judgment.

3. Are Alternative Policy Options Considered? The Supreme Court's decision that NHTSA's rescission of the passive restraints standard was arbitrary and capricious was based on the procedural fact that NHTSA ignored requiring airbags or nondetachable belts, two alternatives. Variations in the passive restraint standard are desirable, but presumably the alternatives would include options other than bags, belts and friendly interiors. Encouraging voluntary purchase of equipment options such as passive belts and large reductions in insurance premiums for safe driving are alternatives to mandatory installation. Mandatory coverage by an occupant restraint would be another alternative; it would allow compliance through several means including the use of manual belts, passive belts, or airbags. Although some alternatives may not fall completely within the purview of the Vehicle Safety Act they may well be consistent with a broader goal of sound, efficient traffic safety policy – something not easily confined to vehicle crashworthiness.

4. Are Nonpecuniary, Nongovernmental Costs Considered? A common imperfection in regulatory decisions is the failure to include all real, social economic costs in benefit-cost analysis and in studies of motorist behavior. There is a penchant for counting highly visible monetary costs. Implicit user costs in the form of discomfort or disutility costs would accompany passive seat belts for some motorists. To these costs time and inconvenience costs would be added in analysis of a policy which requires use of manual seat belts. Inclusion of nonpecuniary costs in analysis of passive seat belts would explain why some motorists will detach the belts and why the usage rate would be greater than for manual belts. Consideration of these nonpecuniary costs would make regulatory analysis more balanced and offer a guide to public acceptance of regulations.

5. Are Interactions with Motorists and Other Safety Factors Considered? An analytically acceptable basis for passive restraints should recognize that, before any requirement, motorists are already making safety decisions and choosing combinations of effort and equipment to produce safety. The individual benefit-cost approach we offered indicates that, in general, the introduction of a requirement for passive restraints will lead to a response by motorists and an interaction with other factors which determine vehicle and highway safety. The interactions can take several forms. For example, if Federal Motor Vehicle Safety Standard No. 208 required that air bags be installed in all automobiles, then a decrease in use of seat belts would be expected as motorists substitute away from the seat belts to avoid the implicit user costs. If the airbags provide relatively less protection in small cars than in large cars, then the decrease in seat belt use should be smaller in the smaller cars. Another form of interaction with mandatory airbags would be a decrease in the value of crash alternatives at bridges as interior protection is substituted for exterior protection. A third form of interaction is the change in motorist driving effort as drivers allow the airbag to substitute for their own safety efforts. Use of the pre-airbag distribution of accidents and severity ignores driver response and nonoccupants and biases analysis in favor of the regulation. This interaction criterion and the other four criteria provide a basis for judging the analytical and economic acceptability of any passive restraints rule.

THE DOLE RULE
ECONOMIC CRITIQUE OF THE CURRENT STANDARD

On July 17, 1984 the NHTSA promulgated the final rule on the Federal Motor Vehicle Safety Standard for occupant crash protection. The standard, which may lead to widespread installation of airbags, was chosen over rescission because the agency concluded that the Supreme Court precluded the agency from rescinding the passive restraint requirement based on existing evidence. The change of position at NHTSA was based on three points:

- as interpreted by the agency, the Court made it clear that the better arguments are those which support increased use of seat belts when passive belts are installed,
- the agency has no new evidence that belt use would not increase, and
- the Court demands a stronger reasoned analysis to support a rescission than it does when no action is taken in the first place.

Instead of rescission, NHTSA chose to issue a rule which is an amalgam of previous rules and new proposals – something old and something new.[25]

The new passive restraints rule requires automatic occupant protection in the front outboard positions in all passenger automobiles by September 1, 1989, with a phased-in schedule beginning on September 1, 1986. The phase-in schedule requires an increasing share of the cars manufactured for sale in the U. S. to have passive restraints as follows: 10 percent of all cars manufactured after September 1, 1986, 25 percent of all cars manufactured after September 1, 1987, 40 percent of all cars manufactured after September 1, 1988, and 100 percent of all cars manufactured after September 1, 1989.

To encourage the use of protection systems other than passive belts , which some motorists may find intrusive, an incentive is offered during the phase-in period from 1986 to 1989. For each car which has an automatic protection system, without passive belts, an extra credit of one-half of a car is given. This credit allows the manufacturer to meet the percentage requirement with fewer cars if something other than passive belts are employed. For example, a manufacturer could comply with the 10 percent requirement for 1986 by installing airbags in 6 2/3 percent of its cars. Air bags, however, are not the only system which is encouraged. There is another system which General Motors has been developing called "passive interiors." Passive interiors build on improved steering columns and padding which may satisfy the injury protection criteria of the Standard. Passive interiors represent a new technology which is recognized by NHTSA as an acceptable compliance method. This technology is being encouraged because it may well be unobtrusive and low cost.

Another new feature of the occupant protection rule is the encouragement of mandatory seat belt use laws. The incentive is possible rescission of the passive restraints requirement. Rescission is promised if acceptable seat belt use laws are passed by a sufficient number of states such that 2/3 of the U. S. population is covered. A state seat belt use law will be acceptable if it meets certain criteria including: a fine of at least $25 for each occupant who does not use a seat belt, and where permissible by state law, a provision that violation of the usage requirement may be used to mitigate damages with respect to any violator who is involved in an accident and seeks to recover damages.

JUDGING THE PASSIVE RESTRAINTS RULE BASED ON THE FIVE CRITERIA FOR ANALYTICAL ACCEPTABILITY

Salient features of this new, innovative, occupant protection standard and its justification deserve comment. The five criteria recommended for judging analytical acceptability, which were presented as questions in the last section of this essay, are helpful.

Are the **overall benefits and costs** considered and are motorists' decisions used as a standard which already incorporates individual benefits and costs? An economic perspective ties these two questions together, but NHTSA treats them separately. The agency does make its own estimate of the safety benefits and the dollar costs, but it avoids addressing the question of the attractiveness of this traffic safety measure relative to other safety and nonsafety activities. An attempt is made to separate valuing the safety improvements from the balancing of the benefits and costs. The notion of valuing accident risk reductions is erroneously relegated to a section on economic impacts where it is discussed along with the nugatory impact of passive restraints on GNP growth. This mistreatment is consistent with philosophical discomfort with an explicitly-balanced safety policy.

On the matter of **motorists' decisions**, NHTSA does devote some effort to understanding what individuals know about passive restraints, what individuals might be willing to pay for airbags, what the relative inconvenience and discomfort ratings are among seat belts and airbags, and what is public opinion on various occupant restraint proposals. There is no weighing of motorists' preferences and potential social problems arising from their imperfect decisions against the imperfect regulations considered. Rather, the focus simply is on public acceptance.

Are **alternative policy options** considered? Clearly many relevant options were considered and several new alternatives are incorporated in this eclectic final rule. Airbags were noted to be the least intrusive in terms of discomfort, but also the most expensive in terms of money. Nondetachable passive belts were considered to be the most coercive and most likely to generate public objection. Detachable passive belts were viewed as being slightly more expensive than manual belts, but also more likely to be used. A demonstration program was thought to be attractive in that it would enhance understanding and public acceptance, but it would delay widespread mandatory occupant protection for years and require legislation for funding. State mandatory seat belt use laws were viewed as providing the greatest benefits most quickly at low cost as long as there is public acceptance. Other alternatives considered were a requirement to offer passive restraints as optional equipment, a requirement for an airbag retrofit capability, passive interiors, and rescission. In addition, as part of the mandatory seat belt use alternative, there was included a change in the law to permit mitigation of damages in civil litigation subsequent to an accidental injury. The departure from a narrow focus on safety equipment is noteworthy.

Are **nonpecuniary, nongovernmental costs** considered? In the sense that public acceptance of restraint regulations is given a great deal of attention throughout the regulatory analysis and to the extent that public acceptance depends on implicit costs incurred by motorists, the nonpecuniary, nongovernmental costs are considered. Juxtaposed to the consideration of public acceptance is the failure to include time (inconvenience) and disutility (discomfort) costs in the analysis of mandatory seat belt use laws. The statement that use "the three-point seat belt" is the quickest, least expensive way by far to significantly reduce fatalities and injuries" reflects this oversight. The contention that seat belt use laws offer safety benefits "with almost no additional cost" is misleading because real, economic costs which the motorist will bear are ignored.

Are **interactions** with motorists and other safety factors considered? Although the answer to this question is "yes and no," the new rule is pathbreaking because of the provision which allows one safety factor, seat belts use laws, to be substituted for another safety factor, passive restraints. It is recognized that the additional safety gains from passive restraints are smaller when use laws are already in effect. In contrast, the agency's analysis is biased in favor of regulation because it overestimates safety benefits. The distortion due to the methodolgy used to calculate safety benefits, a procedure which takes the frequency and distribution of severity of accidents as given. Despite suggestions made during the public comment period, no attempt was made to estimate the changes in motorist behavior involving risk compensation.

From an economic perpective, analysis of mandatory passive restraints should consider the existing, nonregulatory safety efforts. The driving force behind the nonregulatory effort is that motorists themselves have the most to gain and lose in matters of traffic safety. The goal of safety regulation, from an economic perspective, is to improve the decisions made by motorists by helping them overcome any lack of incentives, information, or decisionmaking ability in order to outperform the unregulated (less regulated), private safety market without creating debiliting safety decisions of motorists. The individual decisions already weigh benefits and costs to the motorists and are a standard against which the passive restraints regulation can be judged. Awareness of the information contained in the traffic safety decisions of motorists and appreciation of the tradeoffs which must be made are essential characteristics of any economically sound explanation for a passive restraints requirements.

NOTES

[1] U. S. Department of Transportation. National Highway Traffic Safety Administration. *Motor Vehicle Safety 1979*. DOT HS 805 624, December 1980, page 17.

[2] See U. S. General Accounting Office. *Passive Restraints for Automobile Occupants — A Closer Look*. A Report to the President of the Senate and the Speaker of the House of Representatives by the Comptroller General. CED-79-93. July 27, 1979, pages 6–10 for a history of passive restraints regulation.

[3] See *Federal Register* 42, No. 128 (July 5, 1977) p. 3529 and GAO (1979): 13–39, 76.

[4] Richard J. Arnould and Henry Grabowski. "Auto Safety Regulation: An Analysis of Market Failure" *The Bell Journal of Economics* 12 (Spring 1981): 27–48.

[5] Donald F. Huelke and James O'Day. "Passive Restraints: A Scientific View" in Robert Crandall and Lester Lave, eds. *The Scientific Basis of Health and Safety Regulation* (Washington, D.C.: The Brookings Institution, 1981).

[6] Martin J. Bailey. *Reducing the Risks to Life: Measurement of the Benefits* (Washington, D.C.: American Enterprise Institute, 1980).

[7] John D. Graham, Max Henrion, and Morgan Granger. "An Analysis of Federal Policy toward Automobile Safety Belts and Air Bags." Working Paper, Department of Engineering and Public Policy and School of Urban and Public Affairs. Carnegie-Mellon University, November 1981.

[8] U. S. Department of Transportation. National Highway Traffic Safety Administration. *Final Regulatory Impact Analysis: Rescission of Automatic Occupant Protection Requirements*. DOT HS 806 055. October 1981.

[9] See NHTSA (1981) pages IV-49, IV-71, X-1–13, A-2, A-9 and A-10.

[10] William Nordhaus. *Comments on Notice of Proposed Rulemaking on Federal Motor Vehicle Safety Standards— Occupant Crash Protection.* Docket No. 74–14, Notice 22, May 26, 1981.

[11] For analyses of component interactions see John Hoehn. *The Benefit-Cost Evaluation of Multi-Part Public Policy: A Theoretical Framework and Critique of Estimation Methods.* Ph.D. Dissertation, University of Kentucky (1983) and William F. McFarland, Lindsay I. Griffen, John B. Rollins, William R. Stockton, Don T. Phillips, and Conrad L. Dudek. *Assessment of Techniques for Cost-Effectiveness of Highway Accident Countermeasures.* Federal Highway Administration Report FHWA-RD-79-53. January 1979.

[12] An aspect of benefit estimation which is treated fairly well in three of the four studies is the valuation of increases in safety. Treating risk reductions as if they were infinitely great leads to the untenable position that all government expenditures should be devoted to health and safety programs and risky activity such as travel be prohibited. In this context the appropriate value is the value of a small change in the probability of survival. For convenience the value of this small change is sometimes extrapolated to a unit (1 to 0) change and referred to as a value of statistical life or value lifesaving. An appropriate value of risk reduction based on willingness to pay is used in three of the four benefit-cost analyses of mandatory passive restraints. The values are from $480,000 to $700,000 in 1981 dollars and are consistent with values reported in my survey; see Glenn Blomquist "Estimating the Value of Life and Safety: Recent Developments," in Michael Jones-Lee, ed., *The Value of Life and Safety* (New York: North Holland Pub. Co., 1982). The NHTSA analysis, in contrast, uses a value of $314,000 based on human prediction capacity. Such a practice is difficult to defend theoretically and biases the estimated benefits downward.

[13] The estimate is based on my study, Glenn Blomquist "Value of Life Saving: Implications of Consumption Activity." *Journal of Political Economy* 87 (June 1979): 540–558. Clifford Winston also finds substantial implicit user cost for seat belt use using a different estimation technique and different data. See Clifford Winston and Associates *Blind Intersection: Policy and the Automobile Industry* (Washington, D.C.: The Brookings Institution, 1987.) Chapter 5. For further discussion of implicit user costs see Glenn Blomquist and Sam Peltzman. "Passive Restraints: An Economist's View," in Robert W.

Crandall and Lester B. Lave, eds., *The Scientific Basis for Health and Safety Regulation* (Washington, D.C.: The Brookings Institution, 1981).

[14] U. S. Department of Transportation. *The National Highway Safety Needs Report*. Report to Congress under the Highway Safety Act of 1973. April 1976, pages III-3 and III-4.

[15] See Blomquist (1979) and Blomquist and Peltzman (1981).

[16] DOT (1976) page I-7. Graham et al. (1981) make the same mistake in comparing passive restraints to seat belt use laws.

[17] McFarland et al. (1979).

[18] For a benefit cost analysis of passive restraints which does consider changes in accident chances and implicit user costs see Blomquist and Peltzman (1981). Our study also was available when the Adams Rule was being reconsidered.

[19] U. S. D.O.T., NHTSA *Final Regulatory Impact Analysis* (1981).

[20] *Supreme Court Reporter* "The Automobile Passive Restraints Case." 103, 18 (July 15, 1983): 2856–2875.

[21] *Supreme Court Reporter* (1983) pp. 2856, 2867–2869 and 2871–2875.

[22] *Supreme Court Reporter* (1983) pp. 2874–2875.

[23] *Supreme Court Reporter* (1983) pp. 2871–2873.

[24] Administrative guidance for setting the vehicle safety standards does come from Executive Order 12291, which requires benefit-cost analysis of all major regulations in order to be approved by the Office of Management and Budget. During the Carter administration there was a similar emphasis on regulatory management which promoted a cost-effectiveness. It was ten years after the Vehicle Safety Act became law before limits were explicitly considered on a routine basis.

[25] *Federal Register* 49 (1984): 28962–29100.

CHAPTER 5
IMPROVING TRAFFIC SAFETY POLICY

IMMEDIATE CAUSES OF IMPERFECTIONS

Just as imperfections can be found in the traffic safety behavior of individual travelers so can imperfections be found in the formulation and implementation of traffic safety policy. Vehicle technology has been emphasized at the expense of nontechnological safety measures. Safety of passenger car occupants has been emphasized at the expense of other travelers. Net benefits of crashworthiness standards such as mandatory passive restraints have been exaggerated because safety gains are overestimated and some costs are ignored. The Dole Rule on passive restraints only partly satisfies the five criteria for analytical acceptability.

Such shortcomings might be due to a questionable interpretation of the traffic safety mandate which led administrators to believe that safety gains would be great, costs would be negligible, and public support would be virtually unlimited. As we have seen the safety gains were overestimated. Traffic safety policy was based on several more misconceptions. One was the notion that gains in safety would be had for only a trivial cost. During hearings on traffic safety Senator Ribicoff claimed that a $1.70 safety mirror could make a great contribution to safety. He emphasized that all total the GSA standards would cost only $70 and that on some cars the cost would be negligible.[1] Today the cost of one piece of equipment alone, the airbag, is greater than all 19 of the original GSA standards. At some point the costs become nontrivial.

Another misconception was the belief that vehicle manufacturers pay any costs of the safety standards. Consumers, however, bear part and perhaps even most of the costs. The distribution of the added cost depends on the shift in demand due to the safety standards and the responsiveness (elasticity) of demand and supply to vehicle price. Ralph Nader observed that the gap between existing design and technologically attainable crashworthiness was wide and the attainable level was rising.[2] What he did not say is that if the new technology involves more than a trivial cost and substantial share is borne by the consumer, then additional safety involves difficult choices for consumers, manufacturers and regulators. All are concerned about consumer reaction to the additional costs which accompany the additional safety equipment.

Unlimited public support for traffic safety at the expense of other goals is another misconception. Fragmentary evidence exists that:

- broad support for additional traffic safety action has waned, and
- differences between regulators and the general public exist in attitudes concerning safety regulation.

In a national opinion poll taken for the Council on Environmental Quality interviewers presented a list of ten national problems and asked to which three the government should devote most of its attention over the next year or two.[3] The same poll was taken in three years: 1965, 1970 and 1980. The results shown in Table 5-1 reflect that among such problems as crime, unemployment, education, pollution and racial discrimination, the improvement of highway safety was never chosen by more than 18 percent of the respondents. The greatest support (18 percent) was in the same year of the Senate hearings on traffic safety, 1965. By 1970, 13 percent chose highway safety as one of the top problems, and by 1980 the support decreased to 7 percent. Of the five problems which lost support over the 15 year period, none lost as much relative to the initial level of support (61 percent) as did "improving highway safety."

In another survey, Marsh and McLennan asked: "If you had to choose, who do you think should be principally responsible for ensuring an acceptably safe society for the future — the business community, government, or the individual?" A 42 percent plurality of the public and a 39 percent plurality of corporate executives think that the primary responsibility belongs to the individual. In contrast, a majority, 60 percent, of federal regulators and a plurality of 40 percent of Congress felt the primary responsibility should reside in the government. People were asked also to agree or disagree with this

Table 5-1   RANKING OF NATIONAL PROBLEMS

Question: I would like to ask you which <u>three</u> of these national problems you would like to see the government devote most of its attention to in the next year or two?

	1965 April [1]	1970 April [1]	1980 Jan-Feb [2]	Change 1965-1980 Points	Change 1965-1980 %
Reducing the amount of crime	41%	56%	61%	+20	+49%
Reducing unemployment	35%	25%	48%	+13	+37%
Conquering "killer" diseases	37%	29%	41%	+4	+11%
Improving public education	45%	31%	35%	-10	-22%
Helping people in poor areas	32%	30%	29%	-3	-9%
Reducing pollution of air and water	17%	53%	24%	+7	+41%
Improving housing and run-down neighborhoods	21%	27%	20%	-1	-5%
Reducing racial discrimination	29%	25%	13%	-16	-55%
Improving highway safety	18%	13%	7%	-11	-61%
Beautifying America	3%	5%	5%	+2	+67%
Sample Size	1,500	1,500	840		

[1] Data for 1965 and 1970 are from Gallup surveys. The 1970 Gallup survey was taken immediately after the first Earth Day.

[2] Resources for the Future survey. The number of cases is smaller than the total (N = 1,576) because the question was asked only of a subsample.

Source: Adapted from Council on Environmental Quality *et al.* (1980, p. 7, Table 1)

statement: "Society should restrict certain hazardous activities and products. Even if the restrictions limit individual freedom." The public split with 48 percent agreeing and 45 percent disagreeing, and 7 percent uncertain. Corporate executives were more in favor than the public was with 59 percent agreeing. Again in contrast to the public's position, 87 percent of federal regulators and 70 percent of Congress agreed that individual freedom should be limited.[4] If these two polls are useful indicators, then it is easy to see one of the reasons why traffic safety policy is imperfect — misconceptions.

NONMARKET FAILURE: AN OBSTACLE TO POLICY PERFECTION

A fundamental cause of imperfection in traffic safety policy is the incentive which government policy makers and administrators have to compromise the overall public interest. Incentives exist because public decision makers do not always fully consider all of the social benefits and costs of their action. Traffic safety policy might be understood not in terms of a theory of regulation which prescribes corrective policy for market failure, but in terms of a theory of regulation which explains who wins and loses with certain forms of regulation. Analysis of traffic safety policy using the redistributive approach to regulation might explain, for example, the emphasis on auto safety standards and the almost unbounded support of them by many automobile insurance companies.[5]

Imperfections in traffic safety policy also can be understood in terms of a framework for policy implementation developed by Charles Wolf.[6] This framework also attributes nonmarket failures to misincentives facing public decision makers. But, it focuses on specific types of failures and prescribes that through implementation analysis some policy imperfections can be mitigated. Implementation analysis consists of examining who in government is going to do what and why. Several examples illustrate how this concept of nonmarket failure can be applied fruitfully to traffic safety policy.

One type of failure is redundant and rising costs which we can think of as unnecessary costs. This inefficiency can result from choosing vehicle safety standards over other safety measures because costs borne by those outside NHTSA are ignored. The bias towards technology causes any safety gains to be bought at an unnecessarily high price. In some cases in which excluded costs are considerable, such as compulsory motorcycle helmet use and seat belt ignition interlocks, regulations can even be overturned by Congress.

Another type of failure is caused by organizational goals which differ from higher social goals. One reason for the failure to consider overall traffic safety policy is the artificial division of a comprehensive phenomenon into supposedly separable parts — vehicle safety standards at NHTSA and highway safety programs at FHWA. While division of labor can be productive, in this instance it has led to a failure to consider interactions among vehicle technology, highway design, traffic conditions and the human beings involved in this system. While NHTSA is constrained in promulgating standards for vehicles and occupants, the Department of Transportation has a great deal more flexibility in traffic safety policy.

Unintended side effects, or derived externalities, are another nonmarket failure found in traffic safety policy. The most striking example comes from the review of the evidence on the safety effects of vehicle safety standards. In Chapter 3 we concluded that while overall highway travel is safer, nonoccupants such as pedestrians, bicyclists and motorcyclists are in greater danger. Because the policy approach ignored risk compensation this occupant-nonoccupant tradeoff was unexpected by policy makers.

Bureaucratic blindness covers a lot of problems, but might be used to describe a general failure to operate in the broad public interest. George Eads, former member of the Council of Economic Advisors, gives an example of blindness caused by technological infatuation. He gives an account of the promulgation of FMVSS No. 121 on truck air brakes.[7] The idea for the standard came from the observation that many truck accidents were brake-related and that if the anti-lock technology of the aerospace industry could be transferred then safety could be increased. The information on how effective the standard on anti-lock systems might be consisted of:

- engineering test results on the decrease in stopping distance that could be expected,
- circumstances of truck accidents which relate to probability that the better braking would prevent accidents, and
- the type of problems likely to be encountered in "forcing" a technology.

Eads' assessment is enlightening:

Unfortunately, the bulk of this information was not utilized by NHTSA. Relying almost exclusively on engineering test results, the agency determined to its satisfaction that the standard would measurably improve safety. Only in the

context of an extremely "quick and dirty" benefit-cost
analysis (undertaken, it appears in retrospect, to confirm a
previously made decision to proceed with the standard – not
to evaluate its wisdom) was the second body of evidence [on
circumstances of accidents] tapped – and then only
superficially.[8]

Eads continues by noting that the possibility of problems due to pushing an
untested, complex technical device into the field was not even considered. It
turned out that the field experience with the anti-lock brakes was so
disappointing that some wondered if there had been a net reduction in safety.
Eads' point is that NHTSA had good information, was legitimately criticized
for ignoring it, issued a standard anyway, and that the mistake could have been
avoided in a forthright analysis of the proposed standard.

The General Accounting Office (GAO) gives another example of
bureaucratic blindness caused by excessive organizational loyalty. The GAO
had completed a critical review of the highway safety grant program and sent
its preliminary report to NHTSA for comment.[9] The GAO describes the
administrative arrogance in a way which anyone who has begged to differ with
NHTSA can appreciate:

DOT provided us [GAO] with 44 pages of detailed
comments which it stated represented NHTSA's position.
The detailed comments, for the most part, provided
information on what NHTSA believed to be the true
perspective of the highway safety grant program, which
NHTSA said we had failed to recognize. Many of the
comments were irrelevant because they did not address the
issues being discussed in our report.

NHTSA was not receptive to any of the recommendations or
alternatives presented in the report. However, our evaluation
of the detailed agency comments revealed that NHTSA did
concur with some of our report conclusions, even though
NHTSA generally disagreed with the findings that preceded
those conclusions. None of NHTSA's comments provided
information that, in our opinion, warranted changing our
conclusions, recommendations, and alternatives[10]

It is only natural that an agency protect itself but the contempt which
NHTSA seems to display for both oversight activity within the public sector
and evaluative studies outside of government cast a shadow of doubt on its
commitment to efficient traffic safety policy which increases social welfare.

Such bureaucratic blindness may lead to the conclusion that NHTSA is not promoting overall social welfare, is not amenable to constructive criticism, and therefore should be abolished. On the other hand, if we view these imperfections as aberrations and we believe that the people who make the traffic safety policy and administrative decisions are amenable to suggestions, then we can consider several suggestions. These recommendations follow from the evaluation of policy given in Chapters 2 through 4. They are offered in the spirit of implementation analysis. Nonmarket imperfections are considered along with market imperfections and means for mitigating the effects of nonmarket failures are integrated back into policy design.

CORRECTING POLICY IMPERFECTIONS WITH A BETTER POLICY FRAMEWORK

The chances for improving traffic safety would be enhanced if a less rigid, more general framework were adopted for thinking about traffic safety policy. As pointed out in Chapter 2, the Vehicle Safety Act was based on a mistakenly narrow technological approach which focused on crashworthiness technology and ignored human goals and behavior. A more general individual traveler benefit-cost approach was found to be a better approach because it permits interaction among vehicle technology, traffic and highway conditions and traveler behavior. In this general systems approach, the technological approach is a special use in which travelers are passive to any mandated design changes.

Risk Free Travel?

A supreme advantage of the more general approach is that it introduces explicitly the concept of balance to traffic safety policy. The individual weighing of benefits and costs of additional safety activity is a guide to policy. It explains why attempts to mandate risk free travel are unwise and futile. Risk free travel is an unwise goal because no agency will ever have sufficient power or resources to completely control individual behavior.

Nonetheless evidence exists that NHTSA seriously entertains this risk free goal. Each year NHTSA prepares a report on its activities under the Vehicle Safety Act. Each year changes in the number of traffic fatalities and in the fatality rate (per vehicle miles) are described. Some years the fatalities and rates are up and some years the fatalities and rates are down compared to previous years. Every year, however, the implication is the same: the traffic safety problem deserves more attention than ever before. Travel risks are not zero despite effective policy is the contention. The reasoning seems to be if fatalities and rates are up then more aggressive policy is needed to bring them down, and if fatalities and rates are down, then more aggressive policy is needed to reduce them further.

The individual net benefit approach provides a way of thinking about the costs of pursuing a policy of risk free travel and a way of thinking about a policy risk goal which would reflect social balance.

Inducements and Information — Nonregulatory Alternatives

Use of a more general framework for thinking about traffic safety policy would promote better balance among safety measures also. Since traffic safety is the product of interactions among the individual traveler, vehicles, and highway and traffic conditions, vehicle safety standards are only one of many policy measures which are available.[11] Modern traffic safety policy has emphasized vehicle technology at the expense of nonregulatory alternatives such as inducements and information.

Inducements for Greater Safety

The Dole Rule is the latest form of regulation which attempts to increase occupant protection by legal force. An alternative suggested by the general policy framework is to increase the individual net benefits of protection through inducement. In Chapter 2 we saw that a close and thorough examination of the evidence on seat belt use reveals that people do change their use with changes in the net benefits of use. An alternative to mandatory passive restraints is a program which either rewards belt use or penalizes nonuse. Research by E. Scott Geller, who was supported by the Department of Transportation and General Motor Research Laboratories suggests that even small inducements generate response. The daily chance of (1 in 3,000) of winning a prize valued at $10–$12 over a three week period induced an increase in shoulder belt use from 6 percent to 23 percent.[12] Careful study and planning would have to be done, but a national incentive program with larger rewards might well be a better and more popular buy than compulsory use or equipment. Other inducements such as rewards to manufacturers for sales of comfortable and convenient safety belts or limits to court awards for injury damages if the injured party was unbelted could have the desired effect but might not be as popular.[13]

Despite the rigidity on passive restraints signs exist that indicate a move toward more reliance on inducements in traffic safety policy. The feature program is the anti-drunk driving campaign which was identified by NHTSA and FHWA jointly as one of the accident countermeasures showing the most promise. Accordingly in terms of money given to states under the highway safety grant program alcohol countermeasures was one of the top programs. While past efforts emphasized some sort of treatment for those arrested, NHTSA concluded the new approach would involve substantial penalties for those arrested and a strategy to deter intoxicated people from driving in such a state.[14] The program is designed to provide a greater inducement for safe driving. The program should be evaluated using the general framework to consider all travelers, but there is evidence of safety effects. From 1980 to 1984 the number of drivers killed decreased 11 percent and the number of drunk drivers killed decreased 24 percent.[15]

Information and Inducements — Recalls

Another nontechnological activity which has received more attention in recent years is the safety-related motor vehicle recall program. Since 1966, over 100 million vehicles have been recalled to correct safety defects. The number of vehicles recalled for safety-related defects was 7.2 million in 1984 and it was 5.6 million in 1985. Presumably for approximately half of the vehicles the recall was influenced by NHTSA. Most of the safety recalls are initiated by manufacturers but presumably some would not be made without the requirement contained in the Vehicle Safety Act. The primary source of information for defects is the motoring public who send to NHTSA over 2,000 telephone and mail messages per month.[16]

The recalls provide information to vehicle buyers and users and can help individuals in their own efforts to maintain their desired levels of safety. The information can affect repair decisions and vehicle choice. The recalls can help by providing a greater incentive to manufacturers to build safety into each of their cars. A recent analysis by Gregg Jarrell and Sam Peltzman shows that shareholders of firms whose products are recalled bear large losses. The losses are greater than the direct costs of repairing or replacing defective products.[17] Further study should be done to determine if the safety recall program can be improved, but it does appear to facilitate information flow and provide a greater inducement for safety in vehicles.

Bottom-Line Evaluation

A general policy framework such as the individual cost benefit approach suggests improvements which can be made in evaluation of traffic safety policy. For ex ante evaluation of an single standard five criteria were developed in Chapter 4 for judging analytical acceptability. The criteria cover:

- overall benefits and costs of safety;
- comparison of imperfections in travelers' decisions and regulators' decisions;
- policy alternatives;
- nongovernmental, nonpecuniary costs, and
- interactions among vehicle design, traffic and highway conditions and humans.

Better evaluation at the policy planning stage can improve traffic safety policy.

Bottom-line evaluation is crucial to improving traffic safety policy and must be done in conjunction with ex ante evaluation of individual safety regulations and programs. Bottom-line evaluation means ex ante analysis traffic fatality rates or other traffic outcomes as is appropriate to the policy. Without bottom line evaluation of safety effects no new information can be obtained on effects which are difficult to estimate for single standards. The degree to which a single safety measure interacts with other safety-related aspects — human and nonhuman — can be difficult to estimate. Bottom-line analysis of fatality rates provides information on these feedback effects in the traffic safety system. It also places a check on the aggregate safety impact of individual safety programs. If bottom line evaluation results in an estimated 4 percent reduction in the annual fatality rate, then it cannot be true that each of say 100 different standards and programs reduces the annual fatality rate by 1 percent from the base level.

Given the leading role which trends in the fatal accident rate played in the hearings which precipitated modern traffic safety policy it is remarkably how little effort has been made within the Department of Transportation to understand fatality trends. The record at NHTSA is dismal. An exchange between the GAO and NHTSA illustrates the agency's recalcitrance toward comprehensive analysis of accident rates. The GAO reviewed several safety programs and commented on the lack of analysis of fatality rates. The reply from NHTSA was:

> Unfortunately, the dynamic environment in which crashes occur, the diverse and complex nature of factors contributing to crashes, and the lack of solid empirical data confounded

by factors over which the government has no control, all combine to make it extremely difficult in a truly scientific way to relate combined human factors safety program activities to this illusive "bottom line" of accident reduction.[18]

Only recently has NHTSA devoted resources to monitoring fatality trends. Useful as this effort may be, it does little to improve understanding of the causes for changes in trends. Consider the following statement from NHTSA's First Annual Highway Traffic Safety Trend Report:

> The problem of unraveling various causative factors is quite difficult. Many changes have occurred during the past thirty years, each potentially accounting for either lower or higher accident and death figures. Various changes in those thirty years should auger lower incidence of traffic accidents. These changes include improved roads, better signs, a national speed-limit, higher technology automobiles with built-in safety equipment meeting new standards, the introduction of restraint systems (e.g. seat belts), and the higher costs of owning and operating vehicles.

> But often changes may offset these advances. For example, people are driving more from suburbs to town, families have more cars, the average number of passengers per vehicle is up, density of traffic on the nation's highways is up, there is more driving under the influence of alcohol, and there are both relatively and absolutely more small cars, motorcycles, mopeds, and bicycles on the roadways, all seemingly more vulnerable in traffic accidents than larger vehicles.[19]

The accident factors listed in the report may well be good candidates for determinants of accident trends but there is little in the report which systematically indicates the relative contribution of each factor.

Mystery Plunge

The NHTSA does review trends in fatalities and rates and makes forecasts. The Fatality Prediction Model used is based on a technological approach and is essentially a vehicle mix-crashworthiness model. Factors and their effect on the number of fatalities predicted for 1990 compared to 1980 are: of fatalities relative to 1980 are: vehicle downsizing (+10,000), increase in number of licensed drivers (+5,000), smaller percentage of young drivers (-3,000), increase in vehicle miles of travel per licensed driver (+4,000), increase in highway speeds (up to 5,000), increased use of motorcycles, mopeds and bicycles (+ 2,500), and increase in pedestrian fatalities (+ 500). The forecasted number of fatalities for 1990 is 70,000 up from 51,700 in 1980. The forecasted number of fatalities per 100 million vehicle miles for 1990 is 3.55 up from 3.37. The forecast is described as a strong indication that the traffic safety problem will become more serious in the next decade. The most worrisome problem, according to NHTSA, is the switch to smaller, lighter vehicles which will produce a marked increase in the risk of death.[20]

One problem, as we have seen earlier, is that predictions based on a technological approach are misleading. The positive safety effects of crashworthiness standards were exaggerated. In this instance, the negative safety effects of vehicle downsizing are exaggerated. Travelers will respond to the inherently greater risks associated with smaller cars and partly compensate for those risks. As it turns out the NHTSA forecast was far too pessimistic. Instead of increasing, both fatalities and the fatality rate have actually decreased. In 1982 the number of fatalities fell to 45,779, a level which had not been observed since the energy crunch of 1974–1975. In 1982 the fatality rate fell to (what was then) a record low of 2.88 fatalities per 100 million vehicle miles. The decreases were not one year phenomena. Figures for 1985 reveal that fatalities are slightly less than in 1982 and the fatality rate is at a record low of 2.57.[21] These dramatic declines have been referred to as a "mystery plunge" by traffic safety experts who use a technological approach. Hard pressed to explain the mystery plunge by technological changes they have turned to behavioral changes – changes in driving patterns and seat belt use.[22]

Bottom-line evaluation could take as a starting point some of the more recent models reviewed in Chapter 3 which deals with vehicle safety standards. The model should be based on a general approach such as the individual net benefit model. For short-run forecasts statistical time series models such as a univariate, moving average model. Both types of bottom line models would facilitate overall effectiveness of traffic safety policy. The evaluation would bring together the estimated safety effects of vehicle safety standards, highway design improvements, anti-drunk driver campaigns and changes in human behavior. After the mystery plunge NHTSA researchers, such as James Hedlund and Susan Partyka, have started some bottom-line analysis.[23] These efforts should be developed beyond infancy and integrated into the design and evaluation of each policy action. Bottom line evaluation is essential if imperfections in traffic safety policy are to be mitigated.

NOTES

[1] U. S. Congress. Senate. Committee on Government Operations. *Federal Role in Traffic Safety.* Hearings before a subcommittee on Executive Reorganization. 89th Congress, 1st session, 1965, Parts 1 and 2, pp. 437 and 637–675.

[2] Ralph Nader. *Unsafe at Any Speed* (New York: Grossman Publishers, 1965) pp. 345–346.

[3] Council on Environmental Quality, Department of Agriculture, Department of Energy and Environmental Protection Agency. *Public Opinion on Environmental Issues* (Wash. D.C.: GPO, 1980).

[4] Marsh and McLennan. *Risk in a Complex Society* (New York: Marsh & McLennan Cos., Inc., 1980).

[5] This positive theory explains how some regulatees can even gain from regulation at the expense of some consumers and some producers. See George J. Stigler. *The Citizen and the State* (Chicago: The University of Chicago Press, 1975) and Sam Peltzman. "Toward a More General Theory of Regulation." *Journal of Law and Economics* 19 (Aug. 1976): 211–248. Political theory also offers an explanation for policy imperfections. Interest group liberalism links private group interests to regulation and allows interest groups to acquire some of the power of the state for their own gain according to Theodore J. Lowi. *The End of Liberalism: Idealogy, Policy, and the Crises of Public Authority* (New York: Norton, 1969). The flaw in the pluralist's heaven is that the chorus sings with a strong upper class accent according to E. E. Schattschneider. *The Semi-Sovereign People: A Realists's View of Democracy in America* (New York: Holt, Rinehart and Winston, 1960) pp. 20–43, 35.

[6] Charles Wolf, Jr. "A Theory of Nonmarket Failure: Framework for Implementation Analysis" *Journal of Law and Economics* 22 (April 1979): 107–140.

[7] George Eads. "The Benefits of Better Benefits Estimation" in Allen R. Ferguson and E. Phillip LeVeen, eds., *The Benefits of Health and Safety Regulation* (Cambridge, Mass.: Ballinger Pub. Co., 1981).

[8] Eads (1981) pp. 46–47.

[9] U. S. General Accounting Office. *Highway Safety Grant Program Achieves Limited Success.* Report to the Congress by the Comptroller General. CED-81-16. Oct. 16, 1980.

[10] GAO (1980) pp. 10–11.

[11] The FHWA acknowledges the interrelated system of vehicle, human and roadway environment in their general discussion of traffic safety. See U. S. Department of Transportation. National Highway Traffic Safety Administration and Federal Highway Administration. *Highway Safety '84.* A Report on Activities Under the Highway Safety Act of 1966. 1986, page 68. The fact that two administrations which deal with traffic safety are located in the same Department and use incompatible approaches is an example of nonmarket failure.

[12] E. Scott Geller. "A Delayed Reward Strategy for Large-Scale Motivation of Safety Belt Use: A Test of Long-Term Impact" *Accident Analysis and Prevention 16* (Oct./Dec. 1984): 457–463. For similar results of other incentive programs see *Highway Safety '84* p. 23.

[13] Inducements can be used to encourage purchase of airbags also. United States Automobile Association offers at no additional charge to pay for repair and repacking of airbags in insured cars. For other changes which would induce greater safety see Gerald J. S. Wilde and Paul A. Murdoch. "Incentive Systems for Accident-Free and Violation-Free Driving in the General Population" *Ergonomics 25* (October 1982): 879–890.

[14] DOT. *Highway Safety '84* (1986) pp. 12–13 and 25–33.

[15] U. S. Department of Transportation. National Highway Traffic Safety Administration. *Fatal Accident Reporting System* 1984 DOT HS 806 919 (February 1986). Chapter 2, p. 1.

[16] U. S. Department of Transportation. National Highway Traffic Safety Administration. *Traffic Safety '84.* A Report on activities under the National Traffic and Motor Vehicle Safety Act of 1966 and the Motor Vehicle Information and Cost Savings Act. 1986. Pages 35–43 and U. S. Department of Transportation. National Highway Traffic Safety Administration. *Safety Related Recall Campaigns for Motor Vehicles and Motor Vehicle Equipment, Including Tires.* DOT HS 806 927. For Calendar Year 1985.

[17] Gregg Jarrell and Sam Peltzman. "The Impact of Product Recalls on the Wealth of Sellers" *Journal of Political Economy* 93 (June 1985): 512–536. Also see Steven M. Crafton; George E. Hoffer; and Robert J. Reilly. "Testing the Impact of Recalls on the Demand for Automobiles." *Economic Inquiry* 19 (Oct. 1981): 694–703.

[18] GAO (1980) p. 4.

[19] M. Stern; M. Beauregard, and B. Bragg. *Accident Trend Monitoring and Exploratory Analysis: First Annual Highway Traffic Safety Report*, Vol. I, Executive Summary. For National Center for Statistics and Analysis and NHTSA. DTNH 22-80-C-17062, April 19, 1982.

[20] U. S. Department of Transportation. National Highway Traffic Safety Administration. *Traffic Safety Trends and Forecast*. DOT HS 805 998. (October 1981) pp. 1–10.

[21] For recent figures on fatalities and fatality rates, see Table 1-3 in Chapter 1.

[22] American Public Health Association. *The Nation's Health*. May 1983, pp. 1 and 6.

[23] For an analysis of the mystery plunge, see James Hedlund, Robert Arnold, Ezio Cerrelli, Susan Partyka, Paul Hoxie and David Skinner "An Assessment of the 1982 Traffic Fatality Decrease" *Accident Analysis and Prevention* (August 1984): 247–262. Also see Susan C. Partyka "Simple Models of Fatality Trends Using Employment and Population Data" *Accident Analysis and Prevention* (June 1984): 211–222 and P. P. Scott "Modelling Time-Series of British Road Accident Data" *Accident Analysis and Prevention* (April 1986): 109–117.

CHAPTER 6
SUMMARY REMARKS AND RECOMMENDATIONS

After over a decade of steady decline in the number of traffic fatalities per vehicle mile traveled, the fatality rate increased for three consecutive years beginning in 1961. Traffic fatalities increased by 25 percent over the three year period. During congressional hearings it was made clear to all that traffic accidents were a major cause of accidental death and a major cause of all deaths among children and young adults. The perception that these traffic deaths represented a social problem led to the passage of two laws which are still in effect. The National Traffic and Motor Vehicle Safety Act of 1966 represented the new social regulatory, consumer protection, approach through promulgation of Federal Motor Vehicle Safety Standards designed primarily to increase vehicle crashworthiness and avoid injury due to the "second collision." The Highway Safety Act of 1966 focused on highway design, traffic control and driver behavior using the traditional approach of federal grants to states for safety programs. The mandate in both acts was to reduce the fatality rate and protect the public from "unreasonable risks."

The purpose of this study has been to evaluate overall traffic safety regulation and policy and promote second generation policymaking. Special emphasis has been given to the effectiveness and efficiency of vehicle safety standards set by NHTSA since they represent the new approach to traffic safety. The approach taken was to: develop a useful general framework for thinking about traffic safety policy which includes vehicles, highways, traffic and human behavior; review and critique the evidence on the contribution of vehicle safety standards to changes in the fatality rates; review the development of a specific standard which would require installation of passive restraints and assess the quality of benefit-cost analysis in regulatory and legal decisionmaking; and finally to offer suggestions for correcting nonmarket failures and improving traffic safety policy. The goal is to promote better analysis for today's tougher decisions.

SUMMARY REMARKS

In choosing a framework for thinking about traffic safety policy three approaches were compared. The technological approach views changes in safety as emanating directly from changes in vehicle design. The actual effect of safety equals the intrinsic safety effect in mitigating the second collision. The risk homeostatic approach views potential changes in safety due to vehicle changes as being completely offset by human response unless personal target levels of safety are changed. The individual benefit-cost approach views travelers as choosing safety and nonsafety goals and responding to changes in vehicle design and highway and traffic conditions. The individual net benefit approach is a general approach which considers the whole traffic safety system and which incorporates no risk compensation and complete risk compensation as special cases. After a review of relevant evidence the conclusion is that individual decision makers are not perfectly altruistic, all-knowing and infallible calculators, but neither are they totally unmotivated, ignorant and incompetent; a considerable amount of worth already exists in the individual decisions because they have the most at stake. The individual net benefit approach is the most useful of the three for formulation and evaluation of traffic safety policy.

A cogent question is whether or not the vehicle safety standards produced any safety gains. The claim that any change in the fatality rate must be due to safety policy is shown to be absurd. Instead, the comprehensive studies which estimate the safety impacts of the set of standards on fatality rates were reviewed and compared to the original predictions based on the technological approach. Most of the later studies are bottom-line analysis which employ some variant of the individual net benefit approach. The following conclusions are drawn:

- Occupants of passenger cars are safer.
- Vulnerable nonoccupants such as pedestrians, bicyclists and motorcyclists are in greater danger due to risk compensation.
- Overall roadway travel is safer because the gains to occupants outweigh the losses to nonoccupants in the safety-danger tradeoff.
- Occupants are less safe than the technological studies promise.

The individual net benefit framework was used to review the issue of mandatory passive restraints–a single vehicle safety standard. Critical examination revealed that although the traditional social benefit-cost studies find passive restraints to be a good policy, they are misleading. While benefit-cost analysis can be an extremely useful tool for ex ante policy evaluation, the conventional studies overestimate the social desirability compared to an exemplary benefit-cost analysis. The studies fail to incorporate estimates of the changes in the chances of accidents due to risk compensation and real but implicit user costs associated with passive safety belts. There is great irony in the fact that implicit user costs are neglected in safety decisions even though reductions in implicit user costs (time savings) were part of the justification for building highways in the first place.

Five criteria for judging the analytical acceptability of ex ante evaluation of a proposed safety standard for administrative and legal decisions:

- Are overall benefits and costs considered or is illusive risk free travel the goal?
- Are imperfections in travelers' decisions weighed against likely regulatory imperfections?
- Are alternative policy options considered?
- Are nonpecuniary, nongovernmental costs considered?
- Are interactions with all travelers and other safety measures considered?

The current Dole Rule on passive restraints only partly satisfies these items on the acceptability check list.

Just as imperfections can be found in the traffic safety decisions of individual motorists so too can imperfections be found in the formulation and implementation of traffic safety policy. Imperfections are due to misperceptions about trivial costs of safety standards and unlimited public support. But imperfections are due also to inevitable incentives which public officials have to compromise the general public interest. This nonmarket failure is caused by organizational goals which differ from higher goals. Unlimited side effects such as the greater danger for nonoccupants can result. Through implementation analysis, which involves drawing upon past policy experience, means for mitigating nonmarket failures can be integrated back into policy design. The evaluation review in this book is essentially the implementation analysis. The recommendations which follow are based on the conclusions of the review and analysis.

RECOMMENDATIONS FOR IMPROVING TRAFFIC SAFETY POLICY

Technically a case can be made that traffic safety administrators have done just what was expected of them. NHTSA has promulgated over 50 vehicle safety standards which have enhanced vehicle crashworthiness and NHTSA and the FHWA have provided leadership and funding for state highway safety programs. In this narrow sense they have carried out the specific mandates, described in terms of inputs, contained in the vehicle safety and highway safety acts of 1966. In a broader sense, however, it is less clear that they have carried out the broader social mandate for good public policy free of avoidable imperfections. Based on evaluation of overall motor vehicle and traffic safety regulation and policy several recommendations emerge for improving current policy.

Task Force and Committee on Traffic Safety Policy and Implementation

A task force should be appointed with representatives from the National Highway Traffic Safety Administration (NHTSA), Federal Highway Administration (FHWA), Office of Management and Budget, Council of Economic Advisors and chaired by a representative from the Office of the Secretary of Transportation. The purpose of the task force would be to provide leadership in the development and use of a common general framework for all traffic safety policy, a common set of guidelines for exemplary regulatory impact and analysis, and a common bottom-line evaluation model. After one year the task force would report its recommendations to the Secretary of Transportation.

An advisory committee of outside people should be appointed to provide additional ideas and guidance to NHTSA and FHWA together and to entertain recommendations for improving safety policy. The existing National Highway Safety Advisory Committee could serve as the core of the new committee, but changes in composition should be made to accommodate both NHTSA and FHWA.

A General Framework for Traffic Safety

A general framework should be developed and used to think about all traffic safety policy. The framework must incorporate vehicle design, highway conditions, traffic conditions and human behavior and allow for interactions among these factors in the traffic safety system. The framework must consider the operations of trucks and cycles as well as automobiles. The individual net benefit approach is a good point of departure for development. Such an approach can improve policy formulation, regulatory analysis of proposals and ex ante evaluation of existing programs.

Regulatory Impact Analysis Based on a General Framework

Exemplary benefit-cost analysis should be incorporated into the evaluation of proposed safety measures. Exemplary means that the evaluation is done using a general framework such as the individual net benefit approach and meets the five criteria for analytical acceptability (developed in Chapter 4). Exemplary analysis includes estimates of risk compensation and implicit user costs which are implicitly assumed to be negligible in conventional studies. Initially estimates of the effect of interaction among safety programs and travelers can be based on the existing comprehensive analyses of fatality rates (Chapter 3). Future estimates can be based on feedback from the bottom line analysis done within the Department of Transportation. Exemplary regulatory impact analysis can promote balanced traffic safety policy and give a workable, sensible analytical meaning to protection against "unreasonable risk."

Field Testing for Proposed Safety Measures

Demonstration programs are occasionally developed for safety measures making use of government purchases by the General Services Administration and state police forces. When questions about the additional contribution to safety or the implicit user costs are critical in the preliminary regulatory impact analysis field tests should be made on more representative users. The field tests can be designed to perform a marketing function also. If marketing tests are done for soft drinks surely they should be done for important traffic safety measures.

Bottom-Line Evaluation

More comprehensive analysis of traffic safety measures should be done. The key variables should be traffic fatalities, the traffic fatality rates and the analysis should be based on a general individual net benefit type of framework. Econometric and statistical time series models should be emphasized so as to facilitate bottom line analysis of fatality rates. Bottom line analysis is essential to a better understanding of determinants of traffic safety and taking some of the mystery out of "mystery plunges." Bottom-line evaluation is essential to overall evaluation of traffic safety policy. Bottom line evaluation provides additional information on interactions within the traffic safety system. These interactions are difficult to incorporate precisely in analysis of policy measures evaluated one at a time.

A task force and committee on traffic safety policy and implementation, adoption of a general framework for traffic safety, regulatory impact analysis based on a general framework, field testing for proposed safety measures and bottom-line evaluation could mitigate some of the imperfections in traffic safety policy. These recommendations could improve current and future policy. If improvement is unfeasible, then perhaps policy may be growing into an expensive symbol and perhaps new safety measures should be prohibited. If improvement is unfeasible, then it is time to make once again the paramount comparison between the consequences of socially imperfect decisions of individual travelers and the consequences of socially imperfect decisions of traffic safety policy makers and administrators. Hopefully improvements will be made. Realistically they may not be feasible.

Index